בקול אחד

B'kol Echad: *In One Voice*

OTHER DEPARTMENT PUBLICATIONS:

בקול אחד

B'kol Echad: *In One Voice*

Edited by Cantor Jeffrey Shiovitz
Revised Edition edited by Amy Dorsch

נר ה' נשמת אדם

Published by United Synagogue Youth
The United Synagogue of Conservative Judaism
Rapaport House
820 Second Avenue, 10th Floor
New York NY 10017

A publication of United Synagogue Youth
United Synagogue of Conservative Judaism

820 Second Ave. 10th Fl., New York, NY 10017
http://www.usy.org

First Printing of Revised Edition, 2010
All Rights Reserved

Cover and page design by Dr. Ali Kaufman Yares

Library of Congress Catalog Card Number: 85-62598
© 2010, United Synagogue Youth

REVISED EDITION (2010):

In the mid-1980s when we began to discuss what would eventually become B'Kol Echad, I doubt that any of us realized the impact our discussions would have. Almost twenty-five years later, we have printed, sold and distributed hundreds of thousands of copies. From USY weekends, to weddings, to synagogue dinners, to the Shabbat family table, B'Kol Echad can be found in homes and synagogues all over the world.

For a number of years we knew that B'Kol Echad was in need of revision. Many of the songs we sing today were not in the original edition, while others were rarely used. Revision of the original was a difficult process, because the technology today differs significantly from that which existed in 1986. As a result we had to begin from scratch with every word of Hebrew and English. Although many people contributed to the process with their thoughts and ideas, there was a core group who labored for many hours. Karen Stein, Assistant Director of USY, helped to oversee the process. When Hazzan Jeffrey Shiovitz, the original editor, heard of our intention to revise B'Kol Echad, he immediately offered his assistance. For him, B'Kol Echad was always a labor of love. Proofing this small volume is more complex than one might think. We are particularly indebted to Rabbi Avram Kogen and Hillel Skolnik for their meticulous and steady work which has increased the quality of B'Kol Echad. We are also grateful to Dan Dorsch and many others for their assistance with the proofreading process. We have benefitted greatly from the layout and design skills of Dr. Ali Kaufman Yares, who has helped to give B'Kol Echad a new look. Finally, we must express our gratitude to Amy Dorsch for the many hours she spent on every aspect of this new edition. The love and care she poured into this volume will undoubtedly be returned many times over by thousands of people who will open its pages singing the songs and prayers of our tradition as we "sing a new song to the Lord."

Jules A. Gutin
Director, United Synagogue Youth
April 2010 | Nissan 5770

INTRODUCTION
TO THE ORIGINAL EDITION (1986):

The publication of this *Shiron*, songbook, fills a need that has existed in the Conservative Movement and USY for a long time—to have its own *Shiron* that can be used at conventions, Shabbatonim, meetings and around the Shabbat table. We are told in the Psalms: *Ivdu et Hashem v'simcha, bo-u l'fanav birnana*, "Worship the Lord with gladness, come before Him with songs." It is my wish that through these songs and their singing our tradition will be strengthened.

I'd like to thank Rabbis Paul Freedman and Stephen Garfinkel for their tremendous help in producing this *Shiron*. Many thanks to Velvel Pasternak for his ideas and suggestions and for his permission to use some of the fine translations from his songbooks. To all of the USYers and staff, thank you for your ideas and especially for your enthusiasm. In addition, a special thanks to David Israel (1984 USY International President) for his initiative and efforts on behalf of the publication of this *Shiron*.

Lastly, I'd like to thank my wife and best friend, Robyn, who has encouraged me and helped me throughout this endeavor. I'd like to dedicate this *Shiron* to Robyn and to our new daughter, Rachel.

Cantor Jeffrey Shiovitz

* The translation of Birkat Hamazon which begins on page 47 is based upon a translation originally prepared for USY by Rabbi Robert Binder in 1973.

CONTENTS

ברכות לשבת וחגים

BLESSINGS FOR SHABBAT & FESTIVAL CANDLES

הדלקת נרות לשבת *Candle Lighting for Shabbat*

A minimum of two candles are kindled before sundown and then the blessing is recited. It is customary to cover one's eyes before the blessing is recited. In most cases, we say the blessing and then do the act. However, the act of candle lighting signifies the beginning of Shabbat. Therefore, we cannot light the candles after the blessing has been recited. We light the candles, say the blessing and then uncover our eyes to behold the glow of the Shabbat light.

בָּרוּךְ אַתָּה יי אֱלֹהֵינוּ מֶלֶךְ
הָעוֹלָם, אֲשֶׁר קִדְּשָׁנוּ בְּמִצְוֹתָיו,
וְצִוָּנוּ לְהַדְלִיק נֵר שֶׁל שַׁבָּת.

Baruch atah Adonai Eloheinu melech
ha-olam, asher kid'shanu b'mitzvotav,
v'tzivanu l'hadlik neir shel Shabbat.

Praised are You, Lord our God, Sovereign of the universe, who has sanctified us with God's commandments and commanded us to light the Shabbat candles.

הדלקת נרות ליום טוב *Candle Lighting for Festivals*

(When the festival falls on Shabbat, add the words in parentheses)

בָּרוּךְ אַתָּה יי אֱלֹהֵינוּ מֶלֶךְ
הָעוֹלָם, אֲשֶׁר קִדְּשָׁנוּ בְּמִצְוֹתָיו,
וְצִוָּנוּ לְהַדְלִיק נֵר שֶׁל [שַׁבָּת
וְ] יוֹם טוֹב.

Baruch atah Adonai Eloheinu melech
ha-olam, asher kid'shanu b'mitzvotav,
v'itzivanu l'hadlik neir shel (Shabbat
v') yom tov.

Praised are You, Lord our God, Sovereign of the universe, who has sanctified us with God's commandments and commanded us to light the (Shabbat and) Festival candles.

1

שהחינו *Shehecheyanu*

בָּרוּךְ אַתָּה יי אֱלֹהֵינוּ מֶלֶךְ
הָעוֹלָם, שֶׁהֶחֱיָנוּ וְקִיְּמָנוּ
וְהִגִּיעָנוּ לַזְּמַן הַזֶּה.

Baruch atah Adonai Eloheinu melech
ha-olam, shehecheyanu v'kiy'manu
v'higi-anu laz'man hazeh.

Praised are You, Lord our God, Sovereign of the universe, who has kept us in
life, sustained us, and enabled us to reach this season.

שלום עליכם *Shalom Aleichem*

The Talmud tell us that angels accompany us home every Friday night—both
good angels and evil. When they see the candles lit, the challah and wine and
the table set, the good angel says "so let it be next week" and the evil angel is
forced to reply "Amen." If nothing is prepared, the evil angel says "so let it be
next week," and the good angel is forced to reply with "Amen."

[adapted from Talmud Bavli Shabbat 119b]

Shalom Aleichem welcomes the angels into our homes each week to come in
peace and leave in peace.

שָׁלוֹם עֲלֵיכֶם, מַלְאֲכֵי הַשָּׁרֵת,
מַלְאֲכֵי עֶלְיוֹן, מִמֶּלֶךְ מַלְכֵי
הַמְּלָכִים, הַקָּדוֹשׁ בָּרוּךְ הוּא.

Shalom aleichem malachei hashareit
malachei elyon, mimelech malchei
ham'lachim, hakadosh baruch hu.

בּוֹאֲכֶם לְשָׁלוֹם, מַלְאֲכֵי
הַשָּׁלוֹם, מַלְאֲכֵי עֶלְיוֹן,
מִמֶּלֶךְ מַלְכֵי הַמְּלָכִים,
הַקָּדוֹשׁ בָּרוּךְ הוּא.

Bo-achem l'shalom malachei
hashalom malachei elyon,
mimelech malchei ham'lachim,
hakadosh baruch hu.

בָּרְכוּנִי לְשָׁלוֹם, מַלְאֲכֵי הַשָּׁלוֹם, מַלְאֲכֵי עֶלְיוֹן, מִמֶּלֶךְ מַלְכֵי הַמְּלָכִים, הַקָּדוֹשׁ בָּרוּךְ הוּא.

Barchuni l'shalom malachei hashalom malachei elyon, mimelech malchei ham'lachim, hakadosh baruch hu.

צֵאתְכֶם לְשָׁלוֹם, מַלְאֲכֵי הַשָּׁלוֹם, מַלְאֲכֵי עֶלְיוֹן, מִמֶּלֶךְ מַלְכֵי הַמְּלָכִים, הַקָּדוֹשׁ בָּרוּךְ הוּא.

Tzeitchem l'shalom malachei hashalom malachei elyon, mimelech malchei ham'lachim, hakadosh baruch hu.

תלמוד בבלי מס׳ שבת דף קיט.ב

[Talmud Bavli Shabbat 119b]

Peace be unto you,
ministering angels,
Messengers of the Most High,
the King of kings, the Holy One,
blessed is God.

May your coming be in peace,
Messengers of peace.
Messengers of Most High,
the King of kings, the Holy One,
blessed is God.

Bless me with peace,
Messengers of peace,
Messengers of the Most High,
the King of kings, the Holy One,
blessed is God.

May your departure be in peace,
Messengers of peace,
Messengers of the Most High,
the King of kings, the Holy One,
blessed is God.

3

אֵשֶׁת חַיִל   *Eishet Chayil*

It is customary for the husband to recite the *Eishet Chayil* to his wife before the Kiddush as an acknowledgement of the woman's important position as a mainstay of the household. It consists of the last 22 verses of the Book of Proverbs in alphabetical sequence.

אֵשֶׁת חַיִל מִי יִמְצָא, וְרָחֹק
מִפְּנִינִים מִכְרָהּ. בָּטַח בָּהּ לֵב
בַּעְלָהּ, וְשָׁלָל לֹא יֶחְסָר.
גְּמָלַתְהוּ טוֹב וְלֹא רָע, כֹּל יְמֵי
חַיֶּיהָ. דָּרְשָׁה צֶמֶר וּפִשְׁתִּים,
וַתַּעַשׂ בְּחֵפֶץ כַּפֶּיהָ. הָיְתָה
כָּאֳנִיּוֹת סוֹחֵר, מִמֶּרְחָק תָּבִיא
לַחְמָהּ. וַתָּקָם בְּעוֹד לַיְלָה,
וַתִּתֵּן טֶרֶף לְבֵיתָהּ, וְחֹק
לְנַעֲרֹתֶיהָ. זָמְמָה שָׂדֶה
וַתִּקָּחֵהוּ, מִפְּרִי כַפֶּיהָ נָטְעָה
כָּרֶם. חָגְרָה בְעוֹז מָתְנֶיהָ,
וַתְּאַמֵּץ זְרוֹעֹתֶיהָ. טָעֲמָה כִּי
טוֹב סַחְרָהּ, לֹא יִכְבֶּה בַלַּיְלָה
נֵרָהּ. יָדֶיהָ שִׁלְּחָה בַכִּישׁוֹר,
וְכַפֶּיהָ תָּמְכוּ פָלֶךְ. כַּפָּהּ פָּרְשָׂה
לֶעָנִי, וְיָדֶיהָ שִׁלְּחָה לָאֶבְיוֹן.
לֹא תִירָא לְבֵיתָהּ מִשָּׁלֶג, כִּי
כָל־בֵּיתָהּ לָבֻשׁ שָׁנִים. מַרְבַדִּים
עָשְׂתָה־לָּהּ, שֵׁשׁ וְאַרְגָּמָן
לְבוּשָׁהּ. נוֹדָע בַּשְּׁעָרִים בַּעְלָהּ,
בְּשִׁבְתּוֹ עִם זִקְנֵי־אָרֶץ. סָדִין
עָשְׂתָה וַתִּמְכֹּר, וַחֲגוֹר נָתְנָה
לַכְּנַעֲנִי. עֹז וְהָדָר לְבוּשָׁהּ,

Eishet chayil mi yimtza, v'rachok mip'ninim michra. Batach ba leiv bala, v'shalal lo yechsar. G'malat'hu tov v'lo ra, kol y'mei chayeha. Darsha tzemer ufishtim, vata-as b'cheifetz kapeha. Hay'ta ko-oniyot socheir, mimerchak tavi lachma. Vatakom b'od laila, vatitein teref l'veita, v'chok l'na-aroteha. Zam'ma sadeh vatikacheihu, mipri kapeha nat'a karem. Chagra v'oz motneha, vat'ameitz z'ro-otecha. Ta'ama ki tov sachra, lo yichbeh valaila neira. Yadeha shilcha vakishor, v'chapeha tamchu falech. Kapa parsa le-ani v'yadeha shilcha la-evyon. Lo tira l'veita mishaleg, ki chol beita lavush shanim. Marvadim as'ta la, sheish v'argaman l'vusha. Noda bash'arim bala, b'shivto im ziknei aretz. Sadin as'ta vatimkor, vachagor natna lak-na-ani. Oz v'hadar l'vusha,

4

וַתִּשְׂחַק לְיוֹם אַחֲרוֹן. **פִּיהָ**	vatis-chak l'yom acharon. Pi-ha
פָּתְחָה בְחָכְמָה, וְתוֹרַת	pat'cha v'chochma, v'torah
חֶסֶד עַל לְשׁוֹנָהּ. צוֹפִיָּה	chesed al l'shona. Tzofiha
הֲלִיכוֹת בֵּיתָהּ, וְלֶחֶם	halichot beita, v'lechem
עַצְלוּת לֹא תֹאכֵל. קָמוּ	atzlut lo tocheil. Kamu
בָנֶיהָ וַיְאַשְּׁרוּהָ, בַּעְלָהּ	vaneha vay-ashruha, Bala
וַיְהַלְלָהּ. רַבּוֹת בָּנוֹת	vay-hal'la. Rabot banot
עָשׂוּ חָיִל, וְאַתְּ עָלִית עַל	asu chayil, v'at alit al
כֻּלָּנָה. שֶׁקֶר הַחֵן וְהֶבֶל	kulana. Sheker hachein v'hevel
הַיֹּפִי, אִשָּׁה יִרְאַת יי הִיא	hayofi, isha yir-at Adonai hi
תִתְהַלָּל. תְּנוּ לָהּ מִפְּרִי	tit-halal. T'nu la mipri yadeha,
יָדֶיהָ, וִיהַלְלוּהָ בַשְּׁעָרִים	vihal'luha vash'arim
מַעֲשֶׂיהָ.	ma-aseha.

משלי לא:י-לא

Proverbs 31:10-31

A good wife, who can find? Her worth is far above rubies. The heart of her husband trusts in her and nothing shall he lack. She renders him good and not evil all the days of her life. She opens her hand to the needy and she extends her hand to the poor. She is robed in strength and dignity and cheerfully faces whatever may come. She opens her mouth with wisdom, her tongue is guided by kindness. She tends to the affairs of her household and eats not the bread of idleness. Her children come forward and bless her, her husband, too, and he praises her: "Many women have done superbly, but you surpass them all."

Charm is deceitful and beauty is vain, but a God-revering woman is much to be praised. Place before her the fruit of her hands; wherever people gather, her deeds speak her praise.

Reprinted from *A Rabbi's Manual*, edited by Rabbi Jules Harlow. Copyright ©1965 by The Rabbinical Assembly. Reprinted by permission of The Rabbinical Assembly.

ברכת הילדים   *Blessing of Children*

It is customary for parents to place their hands
on their children's heads and recite the following:

לבנים: *For sons:*

יְשִׂימְךָ אֱלֹהִים   Y'simcha Elohim

כְּאֶפְרַיִם וְכִמְנַשֶּׁה   k'Efrayim v'chi M'nashe

May God bless you as God blessed Ephraim and Manasseh.

בראשית מח:כ   Genesis 48:20

לבנות: *For daughters:*

יְשִׂימֵךְ אֱלֹהִים   Y'simeich Elohim

כְּשָׂרָה, רִבְקָה, רָחֵל וְלֵאָה   k'Sarah, Rivka Rachel v'Leah

May God bless you as God blessed Sarah, Rebecca, Rachel and Leah.

לכולם: *For all children conclude with*
this blessing:

יְבָרֶכְךָ יי וְיִשְׁמְרֶךָ.   Y'varech'cha Adonai v'yishm'recha

יָאֵר יי פָּנָיו אֵלֶיךָ וִיחֻנֶּךָּ.   Ya-eir Adonai panav eilecha vichuneka.

יִשָּׂא יי פָּנָיו אֵלֶיךָ   Yisa Adonai panav eilecha

וְיָשֵׂם לְךָ שָׁלוֹם.   v'yaseim l'cha shalom.

May the Lord bless you and keep you. May the Lord cause the Lord's spirit
to shine upon you and be gracious unto you. May the Lord turn the Lord's
spirit unto you and grant you peace.

במדבר ו:כד-כו   Numbers 6:24-26

From: *Likrat Shabbat: Worship, Study and Song for Shabbat and Festival Services and for
the Home,* by Rabbi Sidney Greenberg and Jonathan D. Levine. Copyright © 1973 by
The Prayer Book Press, 1363 Fairfield Avenue, Bridgeport, Ct. 06605. Reprinted by
permission.

קידוש לליל שבת

Kiddush for Shabbat Evening

וַיְהִי־עֶרֶב וַיְהִי־בֹקֶר:

Recited softly: Vayehi erev vayehi vo-ker:

יוֹם הַשִּׁשִּׁי.

Yom hashishi.

וַיְכֻלּוּ הַשָּׁמַיִם וְהָאָרֶץ
וְכָל־צְבָאָם. וַיְכַל אֱלֹהִים
בַּיּוֹם הַשְּׁבִיעִי מְלַאכְתּוֹ אֲשֶׁר
עָשָׂה, וַיִּשְׁבֹּת בַּיּוֹם הַשְּׁבִיעִי
מִכָּל־מְלַאכְתּוֹ אֲשֶׁר עָשָׂה.
וַיְבָרֶךְ אֱלֹהִים אֶת־יוֹם הַשְּׁבִיעִי
וַיְקַדֵּשׁ אֹתוֹ, כִּי בוֹ שָׁבַת
מִכָּל־מְלַאכְתּוֹ אֲשֶׁר בָּרָא
אֱלֹהִים לַעֲשׂוֹת.

Vay-chulu hashamayim v'ha-aretz
v'chol tz'va-am. Vay-chal Elohim
bayom hashvi-I m'lachto asher
asa, vayishbot bayom hashvi-i
mikol m'lachto asher asa.
Vay'varech Elohim et yom hashvi-i
vay-kadeish oto, ki vo shavat
mikol m'lachto asher bara
Elohim la-a-sot.

סַבְרִי מָרָנָן:

Savri maranan:

בָּרוּךְ אַתָּה יי אֱלֹהֵינוּ מֶלֶךְ
הָעוֹלָם, בּוֹרֵא פְּרִי הַגָּפֶן.

Baruch atah Adonai Eloheinu melech
ha-olam, borei p'ri hagafen.

בָּרוּךְ אַתָּה יי אֱלֹהֵינוּ מֶלֶךְ
הָעוֹלָם, אֲשֶׁר קִדְּשָׁנוּ בְּמִצְוֹתָיו
וְרָצָה בָנוּ, וְשַׁבַּת קָדְשׁוֹ
בְּאַהֲבָה וּבְרָצוֹן הִנְחִילָנוּ, זִכָּרוֹן
לְמַעֲשֵׂה בְרֵאשִׁית. כִּי הוּא יוֹם
תְּחִלָּה לְמִקְרָאֵי קֹדֶשׁ, זֵכֶר
לִיצִיאַת מִצְרָיִם, כִּי בָנוּ בָחַרְתָּ
וְאוֹתָנוּ קִדַּשְׁתָּ מִכָּל הָעַמִּים,
וְשַׁבַּת קָדְשְׁךָ בְּאַהֲבָה
וּבְרָצוֹן הִנְחַלְתָּנוּ.

Baruch atah Adonai Eloheinu melech
ha-olam, asher kid'shanu b'mitzvotav
v'ratza vanu, v'Shabbat kodsho
b'ahava uv-ratzon hin-chilanu zikaron
l'ma-asei v'reishit. Ki hu yom
t'chila l'mikra-ei kodesh zeicher
litziy-at mitzra-yim. Ki vanu vacharta
v'otanu kidashta mikol ha-amim
v'Shabbat kodsh'cha b'ahava
uv-ratzon hinchaltanu.

בָּרוּךְ אַתָּה יי,
מְקַדֵּשׁ הַשַּׁבָּת.

Baruch atah Adonai,
m'kadeish ha-Shabbat.

בראשית ב:א-ג

Genesis 2:1-3

7

Recited softly: And there was evening and there was morning:

The sixth day – The heavens and the earth, and all within them, were finished. By the seventh day God had completed the work which God had been doing; and so God rested from all of God's work. Then God blessed the seventh day and sanctified it because on it God rested from all God's work of creation.

Praised are You, Lord our God, Sovereign of the universe, Creator of the fruit of the vine.

Praised are You, Lord our God, Sovereign of the universe, Who has taught us the way of holiness through the *Mitzvot*. Lovingly, You have favored us with the gift of Your holy Shabbat as our inheritance, a reminder of creation, first among the sacred days which recall the Exodus from Egypt.

You have chosen us of all peoples for Your service, and
You have given us a sacred purpose in life. In loving favor,
You have given us Your holy Shabbat as a heritage.
Praised are You, O Lord, who hallows the Shabbat.

From: *Likrat Shabbat: Worship, Study, and Song for Shabbat and Festival Services and for the Home*, by Rabbi Sidney Greenberg and Jonathan D. Levine. Copyright © 1973 by The Prayer Book Press, 1363 Fairfield Avenue, Bridgeport, CT. 06605. Reprinted by permission.

קידוש ליום שבת   *Kiddush for Shabbat Morning*

וְשָׁמְרוּ בְנֵי־יִשְׂרָאֵל אֶת־הַשַּׁבָּת,   V'shamru v'nei Yisrael et ha-Shabbat

לַעֲשׂוֹת אֶת־הַשַּׁבָּת לְדֹרֹתָם   la-a-sot et ha-Shabbat l'dorotam

בְּרִית עוֹלָם. בֵּינִי וּבֵין בְּנֵי   b'rit olam. Beini u'vein b'nei

יִשְׂרָאֵל אוֹת הִיא לְעֹלָם,   Yisrael ot hi l'olam,

כִּי־שֵׁשֶׁת יָמִים עָשָׂה יי   ki sheishet yamim asa Adonai

אֶת־הַשָּׁמַיִם וְאֶת־הָאָרֶץ וּבַיּוֹם   et hashamayim v'et ha-aretz u'vayom

הַשְּׁבִיעִי שָׁבַת וַיִּנָּפַשׁ.   hash'vi-i shavat va-yinafash.

זָכוֹר אֶת יוֹם־הַשַּׁבָּת לְקַדְּשׁוֹ.
שֵׁשֶׁת יָמִים תַּעֲבֹד וְעָשִׂיתָ
כָּל־מְלַאבְתֶּךָ. וְיוֹם הַשְּׁבִיעִי
שַׁבָּת לַיי אֱלֹהֶיךָ, לֹא־תַעֲשֶׂה
כָל־מְלָאכָה, אַתָּה וּבִנְךָ וּבִתֶּךָ
עַבְדְּךָ וַאֲמָתְךָ וּבְהֶמְתֶּךָ,
וְגֵרְךָ אֲשֶׁר בִּשְׁעָרֶיךָ. כִּי
שֵׁשֶׁת־יָמִים עָשָׂה יי אֶת־
הַשָּׁמַיִם וְאֶת־הָאָרֶץ אֶת־הַיָּם
וְאֶת־כָּל־אֲשֶׁר־בָּם, וַיָּנַח
בַּיּוֹם הַשְּׁבִיעִי.

עַל־כֵּן בֵּרַךְ יי אֶת־יוֹם
הַשַּׁבָּת וַיְקַדְּשֵׁהוּ.

שמות לא: טז-יז. כ:ח-יא

Zachor et yom ha-Shabbat l'kad'sho.
Sheishet yamim ta-avod v'asita
kol m'lachtecha. V'yom hashvi-I
Shabbat Ladonai Elohecha, lo ta-aseh
chol m'lacha, atah u-vin-cha u-vitecha
avd'cha va-amat-cha uv-hemtecha
v-geir-cha asher bisharecha. Ki
sheishet yamim asa Adonai et
hashamayim v'et ha-aretz et hayam
v'et kol asher bam vayanach
bayom hashvi-i.

Al kein bei-rach Adonai et yom
ha-Shabbat vay-kad'sheihu

Exodus 31:16-17, 20:8-11

סַבְרִי מָרָנָן:

בָּרוּךְ אַתָּה יי אֱלֹהֵינוּ מֶלֶךְ
הָעוֹלָם, בּוֹרֵא פְּרִי הַגָּפֶן.

Savri maranan:

Baruch atah Adonai Eloheinu melech
ha-olam, borei p'ri hagafen.

The people of Israel shall observe the Shabbat, maintaining it throughout their generations as an everlasting covenant. It is a sign between Me and the people of Israel for all time; in six days the Lord made heaven and earth, and on the seventh day the Lord ceased the Lord's work and rested.

Remember the Shabbat day to keep it holy. Six days shall you labor and do all your work. But on the seventh day, a Shabbat unto the Lord your God, you shall not do any manner of work, you, your son, your daughter, your manservant, your maidservant, your cattle, or the stranger that is within your gates. For in six days the Lord made heaven and earth, the sea and all that is therein, and God rested on the seventh day. Therefore, the Lord blessed the day of Shabbat and made it holy.

Praised are You, Lord our God, Sovereign of the universe, who creates the fruit of the vine.

קידוש לליל יום טוב · *Kiddush for Festival Evenings*

If Festival falls on Shabbat add this first passage:

On Shabbat, begin here and recite all words in parentheses throughout

וַיְהִי־עֶרֶב וַיְהִי־בֹקֶר: *Recited softly:* Vayehi erev vayehi vo-ker:

יוֹם הַשִּׁשִּׁי. Yom ha-shi-shi.

וַיְכֻלּוּ הַשָּׁמַיִם וְהָאָרֶץ Vay-chulu hashamayim v'ha-aretz

וְכָל־צְבָאָם. וַיְכַל אֱלֹהִים v'chol tz'va-am. Vay-chal Elohim

בַּיּוֹם הַשְּׁבִיעִי מְלַאכְתּוֹ אֲשֶׁר ba-yom hashvi-i m'lach-to asher

עָשָׂה, וַיִּשְׁבֹּת בַּיּוֹם הַשְּׁבִיעִי, a-sa, Va-yish-bot ba-yom hash-vi-i

מִכָּל־מְלַאכְתּוֹ אֲשֶׁר עָשָׂה. mikol m'lachto asher asa.

וַיְבָרֶךְ אֱלֹהִים אֶת־יוֹם הַשְּׁבִיעִי Vay' varech Elohim et yom hashvi-i

וַיְקַדֵּשׁ אֹתוֹ, כִּי בוֹ שָׁבַת מִכָּל־ vay-kadeish oto, ki vo shavat mikol

מְלַאכְתּוֹ, אֲשֶׁר־בָּרָא m'lachto asher bara

אֱלֹהִים לַעֲשׂוֹת. Elohim la-a-sot.

Recited softly: And there was evening and there was morning:

The heavens and the earth, and all within them, were finished. By the seventh day God had completed the work which God had been doing; and so God rested from all God's work. Then God Blessed the seventh day and sanctified it because on it God rested from all God's work of creation.

If Festival falls on another day of the week,
begin here and omit words in parentheses:

סַבְרִי מָרָנָן: Savri maranan:

בָּרוּךְ אַתָּה יי אֱלֹהֵינוּ מֶלֶךְ Baruch atah Adonai Eloheinu melech

הָעוֹלָם, בּוֹרֵא פְּרִי הַגָּפֶן. ha-olam, borei p'ri hagafen.

Savri maranan: Praised are You, Lord our God, Sovereign
of the universe creator of the fruit of the vine.

בָּרוּךְ אַתָּה יי אֱלֹהֵינוּ מֶלֶךְ
הָעוֹלָם, אֲשֶׁר בָּחַר בָּנוּ מִכָּל
עַם וְרוֹמְמָנוּ מִכָּל־לָשׁוֹן,
וְקִדְּשָׁנוּ בְּמִצְוֹתָיו. וַתִּתֶּן לָנוּ
יי אֱלֹהֵינוּ בְּאַהֲבָה (שַׁבָּתוֹת
לִמְנוּחָה וּ)מוֹעֲדִים לְשִׂמְחָה,
חַגִּים וּזְמַנִּים לְשָׂשׂוֹן, אֶת־יוֹם
(הַשַּׁבָּת הַזֶּה וְאֶת־יוֹם)...

Baruch atah Adonai Eloheinu melech
ha-olam, asher bachar banu mikol
am v'rom'manu mikol la-shon,
v'kid'shanu b'mitzvotav va-titen lanu
Adonai Eloheinu b'a-ha-va (Shabbatot
lim-nu-cha u)mo-a-dim l'simcha,
cha-gim uz-ma-nim l'sa-son, et yom
(ha-Shabbat hazeh v'et yom)...

Praised are You, Lord our God, Sovereign of the universe, who has chosen
us of all people for God's service and distinguished us by teaching us the way
of holiness through the Mitzvot. In love have You given us, Lord our God.
(Shabbatot for rest) appointed times for gladness, festivals and seasons for joy,
even (this Shabbat day and) this...

בפסח: *On Pesach say:*

חַג הַמַּצּוֹת הַזֶּה,   Chag HaMatzot hazeh,

זְמַן חֵרוּתֵנוּ   z'man cheiruteinu

Festival of Matzot, the season of our freedom

בשבועות: *On Shavu'ot say:*

חַג הַשָּׁבֻעוֹת הַזֶּה,   Chag HaShavuot hazeh,

זְמַן מַתַּן תּוֹרָתֵנוּ   z'man matan Torateinu

Festival of Shavuot, the season of the giving of the Torah

בסוכות: *On Sukkot say:*

חַג הַסֻּכּוֹת הַזֶּה,   Chag haSukkot hazeh,

זְמַן שִׂמְחָתֵנוּ   z'man sim-cha-tei-nu

Festival of Sukkot, the season of our gladness

בשמיני עצרת
ושמחת תורה: *On Sh'mini Atzeret*
& on Simchat Torah say:

הַשְּׁמִינִי חַג הָעֲצֶרֶת   Hash'mini Chag Ha-atzeret

הַזֶּה, זְמַן שִׂמְחָתֵנוּ   ha-zeh, z'man simcha-tei-nu

Festival of Shemini Atzeret, the season of our gladness

11

(בְּאַהֲבָה) מִקְרָא קֹדֶשׁ,	(b'a-ha-va) mik-ra ko-desh,
זֵכֶר לִיצִיאַת מִצְרָיִם.	zei-cher li-tzi-at mitz-ra-yim
כִּי בָנוּ בָחַרְתָּ וְאוֹתָנוּ קִדַּשְׁתָּ	Ki vanu va-char-ta v'o-tanu ki-dash-ta
מִכָּל הָעַמִּים, (וְשַׁבָּת)	mikol ha-a-mim, (v'Shabbat)
וּמוֹעֲדֵי קָדְשֶׁךָ (בְּאַהֲבָה	u-mo-a-dei kod-sh'cha (b'a-ha-va
וּבְרָצוֹן) בְּשִׂמְחָה וּבְשָׂשׂוֹן	uv-ra-tzon) b'sim-cha uv-sa-son
הִנְחַלְתָּנוּ. בָּרוּךְ אַתָּה יי,	hin-chal-ta-nu. Baruch atah Adonai
מְקַדֵּשׁ (הַשַּׁבָּת וְ) יִשְׂרָאֵל	m'ka-deish (ha-Shabbat v') Yisrael
וְהַזְּמַנִּים.	v'haz-ma-nim.

It is for us (in love) a holy convocation, commemorating the Exodus from Egypt. You have chosen us of all peoples for Your service, and You have given us a sacred purpose in life. Therefore You gave us (with loving favor), in gladness and joy, Your holy (Shabbat and) festivals as a heritage. Praised are You, Lord, who hallows (the Shabbat and) Israel, and the festivals.

במוצאת שבת:	*On Saturday night, add:*
בָּרוּךְ אַתָּה יי אֱלֹהֵינוּ מֶלֶךְ	Baruch atah Adonai Eloheinu melech
הָעוֹלָם, בּוֹרֵא מְאוֹרֵי הָאֵשׁ.	ha-olam, borei m'orei ha-eish.
בָּרוּךְ אַתָּה יי, אֱלֹהֵינוּ מֶלֶךְ	Baruch atah Adonai, Eloheinu melech
הָעוֹלָם, הַמַּבְדִּיל בֵּין קֹדֶשׁ	ha-olam, hamavdil bein kodesh
לְחוֹל, בֵּין אוֹר לְחשֶׁךְ, בֵּין	l'chol, bein or l'cho-shech, bein
יִשְׂרָאֵל לָעַמִּים, בֵּין יוֹם	Yisrael la-amim, bein yom
הַשְּׁבִיעִי לְשֵׁשֶׁת יְמֵי הַמַּעֲשֶׂה.	hash-vi-i l'sheishet y'mei hama-aseh.
בֵּין קְדֻשַּׁת שַׁבָּת לִקְדֻשַּׁת	Bein k'du-shat Shabbat lik-du-shat
יוֹם טוֹב הִבְדַּלְתָּ, וְאֶת־יוֹם	yom tov hiv-dal-ta v'et yom
הַשְּׁבִיעִי מִשֵּׁשֶׁת יְמֵי	hash-vi-i mi-shei-shet y'mei
הַמַּעֲשֶׂה. קִדַּשְׁתָּ הִבְדַּלְתָּ	ha-ma-aseh. Ki-dash-ta hiv-dal-ta
וְקִדַּשְׁתָּ אֶת־עַמְּךָ יִשְׂרָאֵל	v'ki-dash-ta et amcha Yisrael
בִּקְדֻשָּׁתֶךָ. בָּרוּךְ אַתָּה יי,	bik-du-sha-techa. Baruch atah Adonai,
הַמַּבְדִּיל בֵּין קֹדֶשׁ לְקֹדֶשׁ.	hamavdil bein ko-desh l'kodesh.

12

Praised are You, Lord our God, Sovereign of the universe, Creator of the light of fire. Praised are You, Lord our God, Sovereign of the universe, who has made a distinction between the holy and the ordinary, between light and darkness, between the people of Israel and the nations of the world, between the seventh day and the six ordinary days of the week. You have made a distinction between the holiness of the Shabbat and the holiness of the festival, and You have hallowed the seventh day above all other days. You have distinguished and sanctified Your people Israel by Your holiness. Praised are You, Lord, who has made a distinction between the holiness of the Shabbat and the holiness of the festival.

Omit on the last two nights of Pesach:

בָּרוּךְ אַתָּה יי אֱלֹהֵינוּ מֶלֶךְ
הָעוֹלָם, שֶׁהֶחֱיָנוּ וְקִיְּמָנוּ
וְהִגִּיעָנוּ לַזְּמַן הַזֶּה.

Baruch atah Adonai Eloheinu melech
ha-olam, shehecheyanu, v'kiy'manu
v'higi-anu laz'man ha-zeh.

Praised are You, Lord and God, Sovereign of the universe, who has kept us in life, sustained us and enabled us to reach this season.

בסוכה:

*In the Sukkah,
add the following blessing:*

בָּרוּךְ אַתָּה יי אֱלֹהֵינוּ מֶלֶךְ
הָעוֹלָם, אֲשֶׁר קִדְּשָׁנוּ בְּמִצְוֹתָיו
וְצִוָּנוּ לֵישֵׁב בַּסֻּכָּה.

Baruch atah Adonai Eloheinu melech
ha-olam asher kid'shanu b'mitzvotav
v'tzivanu lei-sheiv ba-sukkah.

Praised are You, Lord our God, Sovereign of the universe, who has taught us the way of holiness through the Mitzvot, and enjoined us to dwell in the Sukkah.

Adapted from *Likrat Shabbat: Worship, Study and Song for Shabbat and Festival Services and for the Home,* by Rabbi Sidney Greenberg and Jonathan D. Levine. Copyright © 1973 by The Prayer Book Press. 1363 Fairfield Avenue, Bridgeport, CT 06605. Reprinted by permission.

13

קִידוּשׁ לְיוֹם טוֹב

Kiddush for Festival Mornings

If festival falls on Shabbat add this first passage:

וְשָׁמְרוּ בְנֵי־יִשְׂרָאֵל אֶת־הַשַּׁבָּת,
לַעֲשׂוֹת אֶת־הַשַּׁבָּת לְדֹרֹתָם
בְּרִית עוֹלָם. בֵּינִי וּבֵין בְּנֵי
יִשְׂרָאֵל אוֹת הִיא לְעֹלָם,
כִּי־שֵׁשֶׁת יָמִים עָשָׂה יי אֶת־
הַשָּׁמַיִם וְאֶת־הָאָרֶץ, וּבַיּוֹם
הַשְּׁבִיעִי שָׁבַת וַיִּנָּפַשׁ.

V'shamru v'nei Yisrael et ha-Shabbat
la-a-sot et ha-shabbat l'dorotam b'rit
olam. Beini u'vein b'nei
Yisrael ot hi l'olam
ki sheishet yamim asa Adonai et
hashamayim v'et ha-aretz u'vayom
hash'vi-i shavat va-yinafash.

זָכוֹר אֶת־יוֹם הַשַּׁבָּת לְקַדְּשׁוֹ.
שֵׁשֶׁת יָמִים תַּעֲבֹד וְעָשִׂיתָ כָּל־
מְלַאכְתֶּךָ. וְיוֹם־הַשְּׁבִיעִי שַׁבָּת
לַיי אֱלֹהֶיךָ, לֹא תַעֲשֶׂה כָל־
מְלָאכָה, אַתָּה וּבִנְךָ וּבִתֶּךָ
עַבְדְּךָ וַאֲמָתְךָ וּבְהֶמְתֶּךָ,
וְגֵרְךָ אֲשֶׁר בִּשְׁעָרֶיךָ. כִּי
שֵׁשֶׁת־יָמִים עָשָׂה יי אֶת־
הַשָּׁמַיִם וְאֶת־הָאָרֶץ אֶת הַיָּם
וְאֶת־כָּל־אֲשֶׁר־בָּם, וַיָּנַח בַּיּוֹם
הַשְּׁבִיעִי.

Zachor et yom ha-shabbat l'kad'sho.
Sheishet yamim ta-avod v'asita kol
m'lachtecha. V'yom hashvi-i Shabbat
Ladonai Elohecha, lo ta-aseh chol
m'lacha, atah u-vin-cha u-vitecha
avd'cha va-amatcha uv-hemtecha
v'geir-cha asher bisharecha ki
sheishet yamim asa Adonai et
hashamayim v'et ha-aretz et hayam
v'et kol asher bam, vayanach bayom
hashivi-i.

עַל־כֵּן בֵּרַךְ יי אֶת יוֹם
הַשַּׁבָּת וַיְקַדְּשֵׁהוּ.

Al kein bei-rach Adonai et yom
ha-Shabbat vay-kad'sheihu.

שמות לא:טז־יז, כ:ח־יא

Exodus 31:16-17, 20:8-11

If festival falls on any other day of the week begin here:

וַיְדַבֵּר מֹשֶׁה אֶת־מוֹעֲדֵי יי
אֶל בְּנֵי יִשְׂרָאֵל.

Vay'daber Moshe et mo-a-dei Adonai
el b'nei Yisrael.

14

סַבְרִי מָרָנָן:

Savri maranan:

בָּרוּךְ אַתָּה יי אֱלֹהֵינוּ מֶלֶךְ
הָעוֹלָם, בּוֹרֵא פְּרִי הַגָּפֶן.

Baruch atah Adonai Eloheinu melech
ha-olam, borei p'ri hagafen.

ויקרא כג:מד

Leviticus 23:44

Moses declared the appointed times of the Lord to the People of Israel.
Praised are you, Lord our God, Sovereign of the universe, who creates the
fruit of the vine.

בסוכה:

In the Sukkah,
add the following blessing:

בָּרוּךְ אַתָּה יי אֱלֹהֵינוּ מֶלֶךְ
הָעוֹלָם, אֲשֶׁר קִדְּשָׁנוּ בְּמִצְוֹתָיו
וְצִוָּנוּ לֵישֵׁב בַּסֻּכָּה.

Baruch atah Adonai, Eloheinu melech
ha-olam asher kid'shanu b'mitzvotav
v'tzivanu lei-sheiv ba-sukkah.

Praised are You, Lord our God, Sovereign of the universe, who has sanctified us
with the Lord's commandments and commanded us to dwell in the sukkah.

The festival blessings are reprinted from *Roni V'simchi*, edited by Cantor Jeffrey
Shiovitz, with permission from the Cantor's Institute Alumni Association, The Jewish
Theological Seminary.

קִידוּשׁ *Kiddush for*
לְעֶרֶב רֹאשׁ הַשָּׁנָה *Rosh HaShanah Evening*

On Shabbat, add this passage and all words in parentheses:

וַיְהִי־עֶרֶב וַיְהִי־בֹקֶר:

Recited softly: Vayehi erev vayehi vo-ker:

יוֹם הַשִּׁשִּׁי.

Yom ha-shi-shi.

וַיְכֻלּוּ הַשָּׁמַיִם וְהָאָרֶץ
וְכָל־צְבָאָם. וַיְכַל אֱלֹהִים
בַּיּוֹם הַשְּׁבִיעִי מְלַאכְתּוֹ אֲשֶׁר
עָשָׂה, וַיִּשְׁבֹּת בַּיּוֹם הַשְּׁבִיעִי,
מִכָּל־מְלַאכְתּוֹ אֲשֶׁר עָשָׂה.
וַיְבָרֶךְ אֱלֹהִים אֶת־יוֹם הַשְּׁבִיעִי
וַיְקַדֵּשׁ אֹתוֹ, כִּי בוֹ שָׁבַת
מִכָּל־מְלַאכְתּוֹ, אֲשֶׁר־בָּרָא
אֱלֹהִים לַעֲשׂוֹת.

Vaya-chulu hashamayim v'ha-aretz
v'chol tz'va-am vaya-chal Elohim
ba-yom hashvi-i m'lach-to asher
a-sa, va-yish-bot ba-yom hash-vi-i
mikol m'lachto asher asa.
Vay'varech Elohim et yom hashvi-i
vay-kadeish oto, ki vo shavat
mikol m'lachto asher bara
Elohim la-a-sot.

15

Recited softly: And it was evening and it was morning:

The heavens and the earth, and all within them, were finished. By the seventh day, God had completed the work which he had been doing, and so God rested from all God's work. Then God Blessed the seventh day and sanctified it because on it God rested from all God's work of creation.

On all other days of the week begin here and omit words in parentheses:

סַבְרִי מָרָנָן

Savri maranan:

בָּרוּךְ אַתָּה יי אֱלֹהֵינוּ מֶלֶךְ הָעוֹלָם, בּוֹרֵא פְּרִי הַגָּפֶן.

Baruch atah Adonai Eloheinu melech ha-olam, borei p'ri hagafen.

בָּרוּךְ אַתָּה יי אֱלֹהֵינוּ מֶלֶךְ הָעוֹלָם, אֲשֶׁר בָּחַר בָּנוּ מִכָּל־ עָם וְרוֹמְמָנוּ מִכָּל לָשׁוֹן, וְקִדְּשָׁנוּ בְּמִצְוֹתָיו. וַתִּתֶּן־לָנוּ יי אֱלֹהֵינוּ בְּאַהֲבָה אֶת (יוֹם הַשַּׁבָּת הַזֶּה וְאֶת) יוֹם הַזִּכָּרוֹן הַזֶּה, יוֹם (זִכְרוֹן) תְּרוּעָה (בְּאַהֲבָה) מִקְרָא קֹדֶשׁ, זֵכֶר לִיצִיאַת מִצְרָיִם. כִּי בָנוּ בָחַרְתָּ, וְאוֹתָנוּ קִדַּשְׁתָּ מִכָּל הָעַמִּים, וּדְבָרְךָ אֱמֶת וְקַיָּם לָעַד. בָּרוּךְ אַתָּה יי, מֶלֶךְ עַל כָּל הָאָרֶץ, מְקַדֵּשׁ (הַשַּׁבָּת וְ) יִשְׂרָאֵל וְיוֹם הַזִּכָּרוֹן.

Baruch atah Adonai Eloheinu melech ha-olam, asher bachar banu mikol am v'rom'manu mikol la-shon, v'kid'shanu b'mitzvotav Va-titen lanu Adonai Eloheinu b'a-ha-va et (yom ha Shabbat hazeh v'et) Yom hazikaron ha-zeh, Yom (zichron) t'ru-a (b'ahava) mikra kodesh, zeicher litzi'at mitz-ra-yim. Ki vanu vacharta, v'o-tanu ki-dashta mikol ha-amim, ud-var-cha emet v'kayam la'ad. Baruch ata Adonai melech al kol ha-aretz m'kadeish (ha-Shabbat) v'Yisrael v'yom hazikaron.

Praised are You, Lord our God, Sovereign of the universe who creates fruit of the vine.

Praised are You, Lord our God, Sovereign of the universe who has chosen and distinguished us by sanctifying our lives with God's commandments. Lovingly have You given us (this Shabbat and) this Day of Remembrance, a day for (recalling) the shofar sound, a day for holy assembly and for recalling the Exodus from Egypt. Thus have you chosen us, sanctifying us among all

16

people. Your faithful word endures forever. Praised are You Lord, Sovereign of all the earth who sanctified (Shabbat), the people Israel and the Day of Remembrance.

On Saturday night add:

בָּרוּךְ אַתָּה יי אֱלֹהֵינוּ מֶלֶךְ
הָעוֹלָם, בּוֹרֵא מְאוֹרֵי הָאֵשׁ.

Baruch atah Adonai Eloheinu melech
ha-olam, borei m'orei ha-eish.

בָּרוּךְ אַתָּה יי אֱלֹהֵינוּ מֶלֶךְ
הָעוֹלָם, הַמַּבְדִּיל בֵּין קֹדֶשׁ
לְחוֹל, בֵּין אוֹר לְחֹשֶׁךְ, בֵּין
יִשְׂרָאֵל לָעַמִּים, בֵּין יוֹם
הַשְּׁבִיעִי לְשֵׁשֶׁת יְמֵי
הַמַּעֲשֶׂה. בֵּין קְדֻשַּׁת שַׁבָּת
לִקְדֻשַּׁת יוֹם טוֹב הִבְדַּלְתָּ,
וְאֶת יוֹם הַשְּׁבִיעִי מִשֵּׁשֶׁת
יְמֵי הַמַּעֲשֶׂה קִדַּשְׁתָּ. הִבְדַּלְתָּ
וְקִדַּשְׁתָּ אֶת־עַמְּךָ יִשְׂרָאֵל
בִּקְדֻשָּׁתֶךָ. בָּרוּךְ אַתָּה יי,
הַמַּבְדִּיל בֵּין קֹדֶשׁ לְקֹדֶשׁ.

Baruch atah Adonai, Eloheinu melech
ha-olam, hamavdil bein kodesh
l'chol, bein or l'cho-shech, bein
Yisrael la-amim, bein yom
hash-vi-i l'shei-shet y'mei
hama-aseh. Bein k'du-shat Shabbat
lik-du-shat yom tov hiv-dal-ta,
v'et yom hash-vi-i mi sheishet
y'mei ha-ma-aseh kidashta. Hivdalta
v'kidashta et amcha Yisrael
bik-dushatecha. Baruch ata Adonai
hamavdil bein ko-desh l'ko-desh.

בָּרוּךְ אַתָּה יי אֱלֹהֵינוּ מֶלֶךְ
הָעוֹלָם, שֶׁהֶחֱיָנוּ וְקִיְּמָנוּ
וְהִגִּיעָנוּ לַזְּמַן הַזֶּה.

Baruch atah Adonai Eloheinu melech
ha-olam shehecheyanu, v'kiy'manu
v'higi-anu laz'man ha'zeh.

Praised are You, Lord our God, Sovereign of the universe, Creator of the light of fire. Praised are You, Lord our God, Sovereign of the universe. You have set apart the sacred from the profane even as You have separated light from darkness, singled out Israel from among the nations and distinguished Shabbat from all other days. You set distinction between Shabbat and festivals, filling the seventh day with sanctity above all other days even as You have endowed Your people Israel with holiness. Praised are You, Lord who sets apart one holy day from another. Praised are You, Lord our God, Sovereign of the universe, for granting us life, for sustaining us, and for helping us to reach this day.

17

ברכה לתפוח בדבש

Blessing for the Apple in Honey

On the first night of Rosh Hashanah, after the recitation of the Kiddush and Hamotzi, it is customary to dip an apple in honey and say:

בָּרוּךְ אַתָּה יי אֱלֹהֵינוּ מֶלֶךְ
הָעוֹלָם, בּוֹרֵא פְּרִי הָעֵץ.

Baruch atah Adonai Eloheinu melech
ha-olam, borei p'ri ha-eitz.

Praised are You, Lord our God, Sovereign of the Universe,
who creates the fruit of the tree.

יְהִי רָצוֹן מִלְפָנֶיךָ יי
אֱלֹהֵינוּ וֵאלֹהֵי אֲבוֹתֵנוּ,
שֶׁתְּחַדֵשׁ עָלֵינוּ שָׁנָה
טוֹבָה וּמְתוּקָה.

Y'hi ra-tzon mil-fa-necha Adonai
Eloheinu vei-lo-hei a-vo-tei-nu,
shet'cha-deish a-lei-nu sha-na
to-va um'tu-ka.

May it be Your will, our God and God of our ancestors,
to renew for us a good and sweet year.

קידוש
ליום ראש השנה

Kiddush for Rosh HaShanah Morning

On Shabbat, add:

וְשָׁמְרוּ בְנֵי־יִשְׂרָאֵל אֶת־הַשַׁבָּת,
לַעֲשׂוֹת אֶת־הַשַׁבָּת לְדֹרֹתָם
בְּרִית עוֹלָם. בֵּינִי וּבֵין בְּנֵי
יִשְׂרָאֵל אוֹת הִיא לְעוֹלָם,
כִּי־שֵׁשֶׁת יָמִים עָשָׂה יי
אֶת־הַשָׁמַיִם וְאֶת־הָאָרֶץ, וּבַיּוֹם
הַשְׁבִיעִי שָׁבַת וַיִּנָפַשׁ.

V'shamru v'nei Yisrael et ha-Shabbat
la-a-sot et ha-shabbat l'dorotam
b'rit olam. Beini u'vein b'nei
Yisrael ot hi l'olam
ki sheishet yamim asa Adonai
et hashamayim v'et ha-aretz u'vayom
hash'vi-i shavat va-yinafash.

The people of Israel shall observe the Shabbat, maintaining it throughout their generations as an everlasting covenant. It is a sign between Me and the people of Israel for all time; in six days the Lord made the heaven and earth, and on the seventh day the Lord ceased the Lord's work and rested.

תִּקְעוּ בַחֹדֶשׁ שׁוֹפָר, בַּכֶּסֶה Tik-u va-chodesh shofar, ba-keseh
לְיוֹם חַגֵּנוּ. כִּי חֹק לְיִשְׂרָאֵל l'yom cha-gei-nu. KI chok l'Yisrael
הוּא, מִשְׁפָּט לֵאלֹהֵי יַעֲקֹב. hu, mish-pat L'eilo-hei Ya-akov.

סַבְרִי מָרָנָן: Savri maranan:

בָּרוּךְ אַתָּה יי אֱלֹהֵינוּ מֶלֶךְ Baruch atah Adonai Eloheinu melech
הָעוֹלָם, בּוֹרֵא פְּרִי הַגָּפֶן. ha-olam, borei p'ri hagafen.

Sound the Shofar, on the new moon, announcing our festival. It is Israel's law and ritual; the God of Jacob calls us to judgment. Praised are You, Lord our God, Sovereign of the universe, Creator of the fruit of the vine.

Kiddush for Rosh HaShanah Evening and Morning reprinted from *Mahzor for Rosh Hashanah and Yom Kippur*, edited with translations by Rabbi Jules Harlow Copyright © 1972 by the Rabbinical Assembly. Reprinted by permission of The Rabbinical Assembly.

נטילת ידים   *Blessing for Washing the Hands*

After making Kiddush, we prepare for the recitation of the *b'racha* over bread, *Hamotzi*, by washing our hands. *N'tilat Yadayim* is meant to be a ritual washing and not one for cleaning our hands. Although customs may differ, it is common to pour once over the right hand and left hand and again over the right. The bracha is said while the hands are still wet, following washing or while drying. We refrain from speech between *N'tilat Yadayim* and one's first bite of challah or bread.

בָּרוּךְ אַתָּה יי אֱלֹהֵינוּ מֶלֶךְ Baruch atah Adonai Eloheinu melech
הָעוֹלָם, אֲשֶׁר קִדְּשָׁנוּ בְּמִצְוֹתָיו, ha-olam, asher kid'shanu b'mitzvotav,
וְצִוָּנוּ עַל נְטִילַת יָדָיִם. v'tzivanu al n'tilat yadayim.

Praised are You, Lord our God, Sovereign of the universe, who has sanctified us with God's commandments and has commanded us to wash our hands.

19

הַמּוֹצִיא   *Hamotzi*

It is customary to use two uncut loaves of challah at the Friday evening Shabbat dinner. Shabbat lunch includes two pieces of challah, cut or uncut. At both meals, the challah is raised and the blessing is recited.

בָּרוּךְ אַתָּה יי, אֱלֹהֵינוּ מֶלֶךְ
הָעוֹלָם, הַמּוֹצִיא לֶחֶם מִן
הָאָרֶץ.

Baruch atah Adonai, Eloheinu melech
ha-olam, hamotzi lechem min
ha-aretz.

Praised are You, Lord and God, Sovereign of the universe,
who brings forth bread from the earth.

זְמִירוֹת לְשַׁבָּת   Z'MIROT FOR SHABBAT

Z'mirot are poems sung during the three Shabbat meals which express feelings of joy for the Shabbat day and praise God for God's glorious and gracious acts. The texts were composed between the eleventh and sixteenth centuries under the kabbalistic influences of Rabbi Isaac Luria and Israel Najara.

Z'mirot melodies are usually borrowed from both Jewish and non-Jewish folk songs. Most *Z'mirot* are metric, utilizing the most common of meters. They are sung predominantly in unison, and on occasion, harmony is used.

On Friday evening and at Shabbat lunch, the joy of Shabbat reaches its fullest expression in the singing of *Z'mirot*. These Songs are lively and upbeat to reflect our happiness that Shabbat is with us.

The mood at *S'udah Shlishit* is a more subdued one. Our Shabbat joy is dimmed by the thought that Shabbat will be leaving us soon. The songs at *S'udah Shlishit* reflect this mood and the melodies are quiet and peaceful.

Additional songs for Shabbat can be found in the *Shirim K'tzarim*

(Short Songs) section on page 78.

ברוך אל עליון   *Baruch Eil Elyon*

Each daughter and son who keeps this holy day
will please God in a precious way.

בָּרוּךְ אֵל עֶלְיוֹן אֲשֶׁר נָתַן
מְנוּחָה ❖ לְנַפְשֵׁנוּ פִדְיוֹן מִשֵּׁאת
וַאֲנָחָה ❖ וְהוּא יִדְרוֹשׁ לְצִיּוֹן
עִיר הַנִּדָּחָה ❖ עַד אָנָה תּוּגְיוֹן
נֶפֶשׁ נֶאֱנָחָה ❖

Baruch Eil elyon asher natan
m'nucha, l'nafsheinu pidyon misheit
va-anacha. V'hu yidrosh l'tziyon
ir hanidacha, ad ana tugyon nefesh
ne-enacha?

הַשּׁוֹמֵר שַׁבָּת הַבֵּן עִם
הַבַּת ❖ לָאֵל יֵרָצוּ כְּמִנְחָה
עַל־מַחֲבַת ❖

*Hashomeir Shabbat, habein im
habat, La-eil yei-ratzu k'mincha
al machavat.*

רוֹכֵב בָּעֲרָבוֹת מֶלֶךְ עוֹלָמִים ❖
אֶת־עַמּוֹ לִשְׁבֹּת אָזֵן בַּנְּעִימִים ❖
בְּמַאֲכָלוֹת עֲרֵבוֹת בְּמִינֵי
מַטְעַמִּים ❖ בְּמַלְבּוּשֵׁי כָבוֹד
זֶבַח מִשְׁפָּחָה ❖
הַשּׁוֹמֵר שַׁבָּת...

Rocheiv ba-aravot melech olamim,
et amo lishbot izein ban'i-mim.
B'ma-a-chalot areivot, b'minei
mat-amim, b'malbushei chavod,
zevach mishpacha.
Hashomeir Shabbat...

וְאַשְׁרֵי כָּל־חוֹכֶה לְתַשְׁלוּמֵי
כֵפֶל ❖ מֵאֵת כָּל סוֹכֶה שׁוֹכֵן
בָּעֲרָפֶל ❖ נַחֲלָה לוֹ יִזְכֶּה בָּהָר
וּבַשָּׁפֶל ❖ נַחֲלָה וּמְנוּחָה
כַּשֶּׁמֶשׁ לוֹ זָרְחָה ❖
הַשּׁוֹמֵר שַׁבָּת...

V'ashrei kol chocheh l'tashlumei
cheifel, meh-eit kol socheh shochein
ba-arafel. Nachala lo yizkeh bahar
u-vashafel. Nachala um-nucha
kashemesh lo zarcha.
Hashomeir Shabbat...

continued on next page

21

כָּל־שׁוֹמֵר שַׁבָּת כַּדָּת ·
מֵחַלְּלוֹ, הֵן הַכְשֵׁר חִבַּת
קֹדֶשׁ גּוֹרָלוֹ. וְאִם יֵצֵא חוֹבַת ·
הַיּוֹם אַשְׁרֵי לוֹ, לְאֵל אָדוֹן
מְחוֹלְלוֹ · מִנְחָה הִיא שְׁלוּחָה. ·

הַשּׁוֹמֵר שַׁבָּת...

חֶמְדַּת הַיָּמִים קְרָאוֹ אֵלִי צוּר ·
וְאַשְׁרֵי לִתְמִימִים אִם יִהְיֶה נָצוּר ·
כֶּתֶר הִלּוּמִים עַל־רֹאשָׁם יָצוּר ·
צוּר הָעוֹלָמִים רוּחוֹ בָּם נָחָה ·

הַשּׁוֹמֵר שַׁבָּת...

זָכוֹר אֶת־יוֹם הַשַּׁבָּת לְקַדְּשׁוֹ ·
קַרְנוֹ כִּי גָבְהָה נֵזֶר עַל רֹאשׁוֹ
עַל כֵּן יִתֵּן הָאָדָם לְנַפְשׁוֹ ·
עֹנֶג וְגַם שִׂמְחָה בָּהֶם לוֹ
לְמָשְׁחָה ·

הַשּׁוֹמֵר שַׁבָּת...

קֹדֶשׁ הִיא לָכֶם שַׁבָּת הַמַּלְכָּה ·
אֶל תּוֹךְ בָּתֵּיכֶם לְהָנִיחַ בְּרָכָה
בְּכָל־מוֹשְׁבוֹתֵיכֶם לֹא תַעֲשׂוּ ·
מְלָאכָה · בְּנֵיכֶם וּבְנוֹתֵיכֶם
עֶבֶד וְגַם שִׁפְחָה ·

הַשּׁוֹמֵר שַׁבָּת...

Kol shomeir Shabbat kadat
meichal'lo, hein hachsheir chibat
kodesh goralo. V'im yeitzel chovat
hayom ashrei lo, l'Eil adon
m'chol'lo, mincha hi sh'lucha.

Hashomeir Shabbat...

Chemdat hayamim k'ra-o Eili tzur,
v'ashrei litmimim im yihyeh natzur.
Keter hilumim al rosham yatzur,
tzur ha-olamin rucho bam nacha.

Hashomeir Shabbat...

Zachor et yom HaShabbat l'kad'sho,
karno ki gavha neizer al rosho,
Al kein yitein ha-adam l'nafsho
Oneg v'gam simcha bahem lo
l'moshcha.

Hashomeir Shabbat...

Kodesh hi lachem Shabbat hamalka,
El toch bateichem l'hani-ach b'racha.
B'chol moshvoteichem lo ta-asu
m'lacha, B'neichem uv-noteichem,
eved v'gam shifcha.

Hashomeir Shabbat...

Blessed is God on high who gave rest, relief for the soul with woe oppressed. and God will demand for Zion distressed, "How long will this soul its suffering feel?"

Each daughter and son who keeps holy this day
will please the Lord in a precious way.

The Ruler in Heaven, our Sovereign most great commanded God's people to cherish this date: make Shabbat a joy with good food on the plate, with handsome clothes and the family meal.

Each daughter and son...

O keep the Shabbat in rest and delight, and soon you will love what is holy and right; a blessing to keep it with all your might—the Creator is pleased at this goodly zeal.

Each daughter and son...

My Ruler has called it the choicest of days; happy the faithful who keep it always: a crowning reward will God give them in praise with them will God dwell, to bless and to heal.

Each daughter and son...

Remember: holy must the Shabbat be, crowned in its glory with majesty; so let a person have pleasure, rest free: This day, for joy, like a king let him feel.

Each daughter and son...

Let Shabbat the Queen be holy for you, to leave her blessing in your home too; wherever you live, no work shall you do— nor children, or servant with whom you deal.

Each daughter and son...

Rabbi Baruch ben Shmuel of Mayence

Note: *The acrostic spells out "Baruch Chazak" could be the author's "signature." In contemporary times, the "Baruch Chazak" could also be attributed to commending strength.*

At Shabbat lunch, the mood of the *z'mirot* is also upbeat, lively and joyful.
Shabbat is in full swing and the z'mirot and their melodies reflect this joy.

דרור יקרא   *D'ror Yikra*

Shabbat is a day of freedom, God will help us overcome our enemies

דְּרוֹר יִקְרָא לְבֵן וּלְבַת	D'ror yikra l'vein ul-vat,
וְיִנְצָרְכֶם כְּמוֹ בָבַת	v'yin-tzor-chem k'mo vavat,
נְעִים שִׁמְכֶם וְלֹא יֻשְׁבַּת	n'im shimchem v'lo yushbat,
שְׁבוּ וְנוּחוּ בְּיוֹם שַׁבָּת	sh'vu v'nuchu b'yom Shabbat.
דְּרוֹשׁ נָוִי וְאוּלַמִּי	D'rosh navi v'ulami,
וְאוֹת יֶשַׁע עֲשֵׂה עִמִּי	v'ot yesha asei imi,
נְטַע שׂוֹרֵק בְּתוֹךְ כַּרְמִי	n'ta soreik b'toch karmi,
שְׁעֵה שַׁוְעַת בְּנֵי עַמִּי	sh'ei shav'at b'nei ami.
דְּרוֹךְ פּוּרָה בְּתוֹךְ בָּצְרָה	D'roch pura b'toch batzra,
וְגַם בָּבֶל אֲשֶׁר גָּבְרָה	v'gam bevel asher gav'ra,
נְתוֹץ צָרַי בְּאַף עֶבְרָה	n'totz tzarai b'af evra,
שְׁמַע קוֹלִי בְּיוֹם אֶקְרָא	s'hma k'oli b'yom ekra.
אֱלֹהִים תֵּן בְּמִדְבָּר הַר	Elohim tein b'midbar har,
הֲדַס שִׁטָּה בְּרוֹשׁ תִּדְהָר	hadas shita b'rosh tidhar,
וְלַמַּזְהִיר וְלַנִּזְהָר	v'lamaz-hir v'laniz-har,
שְׁלוֹמִים תֵּן כְּמֵי נָהָר	sh'lomim tein k'mei nahar.
הֲדוֹךְ קָמַי, אֵל קַנָּא	Hadoch kamai, Eil kana,
בְּמוֹג לֵבָב וּבִמְגִנָּה	b'mog leivav uvam'gina,
וְנַרְחִיב פֶּה וּנְמַלְאֶנָּא	v'nar-chiv peh un'mal'ehna,
לְשׁוֹנֵנוּ לְךָ רִנָּה	l'shoneinu l'cha rina.
דְּעֵה חָכְמָה לְנַפְשֶׁךָ	D'ei chochma l'nafshecha,
וְהִיא כֶתֶר לְרֹאשֶׁךָ	v'hi cheter l'roshecha,
נְצֹר מִצְוַת קְדוֹשֶׁךָ	n'tzor mitzvat k'doshecha,
שְׁמוֹר שַׁבַּת קָדְשֶׁךָ	sh'mor Shabbat kodshecha

24

God will proclaim freedom for all of God's children
And will keep you as the apple of God's eye
Pleasant is your name and will not be destroyed
Repose and rest on Shabbat.

Seek my sanctuary and my home
Give me a sign of deliverance
Plant a vine in my vineyard
Look to my people, hear their laments.

Tread the wine-press in Bozrah,
And in Babylon that city of might
Crush my enemies in anger and fury
On the day when I cry, hear my voice.

Plant, O God, in the mountain waste
Fir and acacia, myrtle and elm
Give those who teach and those who obey
Abundant peace, like the flow of a river.

Respect my enemies, O zealous God
Fill their hearts with fear and despair
Then we shall open our mouths,
And fill our tongues with Your praise.

Know wisdom, that your soul may live,
And it shall be a diadem for your brow
Keep the commandment of your Holy One
Observe Shabbat, your sacred day.

The acrostic gives the name Dunash, whom several authorities identify as
Dunash ibn Labrat, who lived in the 10th century in Baghdad and Cordova

כִּי אֶשְׁמְרָה שַׁבָּת *Ki Eshmera Shabbat*

Shabbat as a bond between God and the Jewish people

כִּי אֶשְׁמְרָה שַׁבָּת אֵל יִשְׁמְרֵנִי

Ki eshmera Shabbat Eil yishme-reini

אוֹת הִיא לְעוֹלְמֵי עַד
בֵּינוֹ וּבֵינִי.

ot hee l'olmei ad
beino oo-veini.

אָסוּר מְצֹא חֵפֶץ עֲשׂוֹת דְּרָכִים
גַּם מִלְּדַבֵּר בּוֹ דִּבְרֵי צְרָכִים
דִּבְרֵי סְחוֹרָה אַף דִּבְרֵי מְלָכִים
אֶהֱגֶה בְּתוֹרַת אֵל וּתְחַכְּמֵנִי

Asur m'tzo cheifetz asot d'rachim.
Gam mil-dabeir bo divrei tz'rachim,
divrei s'chora af divrei m'lachim,
Eh-he-ge b'torat Eil ut'chakmeini.

אוֹת הִיא לְעוֹלְמֵי עַד
בֵּינוֹ וּבֵינִי.

ot hee l'olmei ad
beino oo-veini.

בּוֹ אֶמְצָא תָּמִיד נֹפֶשׁ לְנַפְשִׁי
הִנֵּה לְדוֹר רִאשׁוֹן נָתַן קְדֹשִׁי
מוֹפֵת בְּתֵת לֶחֶם מִשְׁנֶה בַּשִּׁשִּׁי
כָּכָה בְּכָל-שִׁשִּׁי יַכְפִּיל מְזוֹנִי

Bo em-tzah tamid nofesh l'nafshi,
Hinei l'dor rishon natan k'doshi,
Mofeit b'teit lechem mishneh b'shishi
kacha b'chol shishi yach-pil m'zoni.

אוֹת הִיא לְעוֹלְמֵי עַד
בֵּינוֹ וּבֵינִי.

ot hee l'olmei ad
beino oo-veini.

רָשַׁם בְּדָת הָאֵל חֹק אֶל סְגָנָיו
בּוֹ לַעֲרֹךְ לֶחֶם פָּנִים לְפָנָיו עַל
כֵּן לְהִתְעַנּוֹת בּוֹ עַל פִּי נְבוֹנָיו
אָסוּר לְבַד מִיּוֹם כִּפּוּר עֲוֹנִי

Rasham b'dat ha-el chok el s'ganav
bo la-aroch lechem panim b'fanav al
kein l'hitanot bo al pi n'vonav.
asur l'vad mi-yom kippur ah-voni.

אוֹת הִיא לְעוֹלְמֵי עַד
בֵּינוֹ וּבֵינִי.

ot hee l'olmei ad
beino oo-veini.

הוּא יוֹם מְכֻבָּד; הוּא יוֹם
תַּעֲנוּגִים לֶחֶם וְיַיִן טוֹב, בָּשָׂר
וְדָגִים הַמִּתְאַבְּלִים בּוֹ אָחוֹר

Hu yom m'chubad; hu yom
ta-anugim. Lechem v'yayin tov, basar
v'dagim. Hamitablim bo, achor

נְסוֹגִים ✦ כִּי יוֹם שְׂמָחוֹת הוּא
וּתְשַׂמְּחֵנִי ✦

אוֹת הִיא לְעוֹלְמֵי עַד
בֵּינוֹ וּבֵינִי.

מֵחֵל מְלָאכָה בּוֹ סוֹפוֹ לְהַכְרִית ✦
עַל כֵּן אֲכַבֶּס־בּוֹ לִבִּי כְּבֹרִית ✦
וְאֶתְפַּלְּלָה אֶל אֵל עַרְבִית
וְשַׁחֲרִית ✦

מוּסָף וְגַם מִנְחָה הוּא יַעֲנֵנִי
אוֹת הִיא לְעוֹלְמֵי עַד
בֵּינוֹ וּבֵינִי.

n'sogim Ki yom s'machot hu
ut-sam-cheini.

ot hcc l'olmei ad
beino oo-veini.

Mechel m'l'acha bo, sofo L'hachrit,
al kein achabeis bo Libi k'vorit,
v'etpal'la el Eil arvit
v'shacharit,
musaf v'gam mincha hu ya-aneini.

ot hee l'olmei ad
beino oo-veini.

As I observe Shabbat, God watches over me.
It is a sign forever between God and me.

Composed by Avraham Ibn Ezra

The first letter of each verse of this *zemer* forms the first name of the author, Avraham Ibn Ezra. In this song, we ask God to watch over us and remember Shabbat as a sign between God and the Jewish people. Shabbat rituals, customs and legalities are illustrated such as *lechem mishneh*, the double portion of *challah* found on every Shabbat table, studying Torah, and the enjoyment of good food.

By mentioning rituals, customs and *halachik* requirements, we are reminded to make Shabbat distinct, to mark it as a holy day through meaningful actions and *mitzvot* that connect us with God.

27

מַה יְדִידוּת *Mah Y'didut*

Shabbat as a day of *oneg* or joy

מַה־יְדִידוּת מְנוּחָתֵךְ ּ	Mah y'didut m'nuchateich,
אַתְּ שַׁבָּת הַמַּלְכָּה ּ	at Shabbat hamalka,
בְּכֵן נָרוּץ לִקְרָאתֵךְ ּ	b'chein narutz likrateich,
בּוֹאִי כַלָּה נְסוּכָה ּ	bo-i challah n'sucha,
לְבוּשׁ בִּגְדֵי חֲמוּדוֹת ּ	l'vush bigdei chamudot,
לְהַדְלִיק נֵר בִּבְרָכָה ּ	l'hadlik neir bivracha,
וַתֵּכֶל כָּל הָעֲבוֹדוֹת ּ	Vateichel kol ha-avodot,
לֹא תַעֲשׂוּ מְלָאכָה ּ	lo ta-asu m'lacha.
לְהִתְעַנֵּג בְּתַעֲנוּגִים	*L'hitaneig b'ta-anugim*
בַּרְבּוּרִים וּשְׂלָו וְדָגִים ּ	*barburim us-lav v'dagim.*

מֵעֶרֶב מַזְמִינִים ּ	Mei-erev mazminim,
כָּל־מִינֵי מַטְעַמִּים ּ	kol minei matamin,
מִבְּעוֹד יוֹם מוּכָנִים ּ	mib'od yom muchanim,
תַּרְנְגוֹלִים מְפֻטָּמִים ּ	tarn'golim m'futamin.
וְלַעֲרֹךְ כַּמָּה מִינִים ּ	v'la-aroch kama minim
שְׁתוֹת יֵינוֹת מְבֻשָּׂמִים ּ	sh'tot yeinot m'vusamim,
וְתַפְנוּקֵי מַעֲדַנִּים,	v'taf-nukei ma-a-danim
בְּכָל־שָׁלוֹשׁ פְּעָמִים	b'chol shalosh p'amim.
לְהִתְעַנֵּג בְּתַעֲנוּגִים בַּרְבּוּרִים...	*L'hitaneig b'ta-anugim barburim...*

נַחֲלַת יַעֲקֹב יִירָשׁ ּ	Nachalat Ya-akov yirash,
בְּלִי מְצָרִים נַחֲלָה ּ	b'li m'tzarim nacha-la,
וִיכַבְּדוּהוּ עָשִׁיר וָרָשׁ ּ	viychab'duhu ashir varash
וְתִזְכּוּ לִגְאֻלָּה ּ	v'tizku lig-ula,
יוֹם שַׁבָּת אִם תְּכַבְּדוּ	Yom Shabbat im t'chabdu,
וִהְיִיתֶם לִי סְגֻלָּה,	vi-yiten li s'gula,
שֵׁשֶׁת יָמִים תַּעֲבֹדוּ ּ	sheishet yamin ta-avodu
וּבַשְּׁבִיעִי נָגִילָה ּ	u-vash'vi-i nagila.

28

לְהִתְעַנֵּג בְּתַעֲנוּגִים בַּרְבּוּרִים...	*L'hitaneig b'ta-anugim barburim...*
חֲפָצֶיךָ אֲסוּרִים ❖	Chafatzecha asurim
❖ וְגַם לַחֲשֹׁב חֶשְׁבּוֹנוֹת	v'gam lachashov cheshbonot,
הִרְהוּרִים מֻתָּרִים ❖	hirhurim mutarim
וּלְשַׁדֵּךְ הַבָּנוֹת ❖	ul-shadeich habanot,
וְתִינוֹק לְלַמְּדוֹ סֵפֶר ❖	v'tinok l'lamdo seifer,
לַמְנַצֵּחַ בִּנְגִינוֹת ❖	lam'natzei-ach bin-ginot,
וְלַהֲגוֹת בְּאִמְרֵי־שֶׁפֶר ❖	v'la-hagot b'imrei shefer
בְּכָל־פִּנּוֹת וּמַחֲנוֹת ❖	b'chol pinot u'machanot.
לְהִתְעַנֵּג בְּתַעֲנוּגִים בַּרְבּוּרִים...	*L'hitaneig b'ta-anugim barburim...*
הִלּוּכְךָ יְהִי בְנַחַת ❖	Hiluchach y'hi v'nachat,
עֹנֶג קְרָא לַשַּׁבָּת ❖	oneg k'ra laShabbat,
וְהַשֵּׁנָה מְשֻׁבַּחַת ❖	v'hasheina m'shubachat
כְּדָת נֶפֶשׁ מְשִׁיבַת ❖	k'dat nefesh m'shivat,
בְּכֵן נַפְשִׁי לְךָ עָרְגָה ❖	b'chein nafshi l'cha arga
וְלָנוּחַ בְּחִבַּת ❖	v'lanuach b'chibat,
כַּשׁוֹשַׁנִּים סוּגָה ❖	kashoshanim suga
בּוֹ יָנוּחוּ בֵּן וּבַת ❖	bo yanuchu bein u-vat.
לְהִתְעַנֵּג בְּתַעֲנוּגִים בַּרְבּוּרִים...	*L'hitaneig b'ta-anugim barburim...*
מֵעֵין עוֹלָם הַבָּא ❖	Mei-ein olam haba
יוֹם שַׁבָּת מְנוּחָה ❖	yom shabbat m'nucha,
כָּל־הַמִּתְעַנְּגִים בָּהּ ❖	kol hamitan'gim ba
יִזְכּוּ לְרֹב שִׂמְחָה ❖	yizku l'rov simcha,
מֵחֶבְלֵי מָשִׁיחַ ❖	mei-chevlei Mashiach
יֻצָּלוּ לִרְוָחָה ❖	yu-tzalu lirvacha,
פְּדוּתֵנוּ תַצְמִיחַ ❖	p'duteinu tatzmiach
וְנָס יָגוֹן וַאֲנָחָה ❖	v'nas yagon va-anacha.
לְהִתְעַנֵּג בְּתַעֲנוּגִים בַּרְבּוּרִים...	*L'hitaneig b'ta-anugim barburim...*

How beloved is your rest!
You are Shabbat, the Queen!
Therefore we will run to greet you.
O, come! Anointed bride!
Dressed in fine clothing
We will light the candles with a b'racha.
All work has ceased.
For it is written: "You shall not do any work."

(It is a time) to delight in all kinds of pleasures: fatted geese, quail, and fish.

From the day before Shabbat
All kinds of delicious foods are prepared.
On Friday itself, fattened chickens are made ready.
We set the table with all kinds of foods
And we drink sweet-smelling wines.
We enjoy delicacies at all three meals.

(It is a time) to delight in all kinds of pleasures: fatted geese, quail, and fish.

The heritage of Jacob will be inherited;
it is a heritage without borders.
Both rich and poor shall honor Shabbat
and will thus merit redemption.
If you honor the day of Shabbat
(God says:) "You shall be for Me as a treasured possession."

(It is a time) to delight in all kinds of pleasures: fatted geese, quail, and fish.

Taking care of business matters is forbidden
as is figuring out accounts.
It is permissible to think about such things
as it is to arrange marriages.
(So too is it permitted) to teach a child a book
and to sing melodies,
and to speak good words (of Torah)
in all corners and places.

(It is a time) to delight in all kinds of pleasures: fatted geese, quail, and fish.

You should walk at a slow pace
And you shall call the Shabbat "a joy."
Sleeping is praiseworthy for it restores the soul.
Therefore my soul longs for you, Shabbat,
To rest in love.
(Shabbat is a day) that is fenced about by lilies;
On that day shall son and daughter rest.

(It is a time) to delight in all kinds of pleasures: fatted geese, quail, and fish.

Shabbat, the day of rest is a taste of the World to Come.
All those who enjoy themselves on this day
shall merit much happiness.
They shall be saved from suffering
that will precede the coming of the Messiah.
Our redemption will flourish
and all grief and sorrow will disappear.

(It is a time) to delight in all kinds of pleasures: fatted geese, quail, and fish.

Attributed to Menachem ben Machir of Ratisbone

From *Ma Y'didut*. Copyright © 1979 by Leaders Training Fellowship of The Jewish Theological Seminary. Reprinted by permission.

מנוחה ושמחה　Menucha V'simcha

Shabbat as a day for rest and happiness

מְנוּחָה וְשִׂמְחָה אוֹר לַיְּהוּדִים ⋄	M'nucha v'simcha or lay'hudim,
יוֹם שַׁבָּתוֹן יוֹם מַחֲמַדִּים ⋄	Yom Shabbaton yom machamadim.
שׁוֹמְרָיו וְזוֹכְרָיו הֵמָּה מְעִידִים ⋄	shomrav v'zochrav heima m'idim,
כִּי לְשִׁשָּׁה כֹּל בְּרוּאִים וְעוֹמְדִים ⋄	ki l'shisha kol b'ru-im v'omdim.

שְׁמֵי שָׁמַיִם אֶרֶץ וְיַמִּים ⋄	Sh'mei shamayim eretz v'yamim,
כָּל־צְבָא מָרוֹם גְּבוֹהִים וְרָמִים ⋄	kol tz'va marom g'vohim v'ramim,
תַּנִּין וְאָדָם וְחַיַּת רְאֵמִים ⋄	tanim v'adam v'chayat r'eimim,
כִּי בְּיָהּ יי צוּר עוֹלָמִים ⋄	ki b'yah Adonai tzur olamim.

הוּא אֲשֶׁר דִּבֶּר לְעַם סְגֻלָּתוֹ ⋄	Hu asher diber l'am s'gulato,
שָׁמוֹר לְקַדְּשׁוֹ מִבּוֹאוֹ וְעַד צֵאתוֹ ⋄	shamor l'kad'sho mibo'oh v'ad tzeito,
שַׁבַּת קֹדֶשׁ יוֹם חֶמְדָּתוֹ ⋄	Shabbat kodesh yom chemdato,
כִּי בוֹ שָׁבַת מִכָּל־מְלַאכְתּוֹ ⋄	ki vo shavat mikol m'lachto.

שְׁמֵי שָׁמַיִם...　*Sh'mei shamayim eretz v'yamin...*

בְּמִצְוַת שַׁבָּת אֵל יַחֲלִיצָךְ ⋄	B'mitzvat Shabbat eil yachalitzach,
קוּם קְרָא אֵלָיו יָחִישׁ לְאַמְּצָךְ ⋄	kum k'ra eilav yachish l'amtzach.
נִשְׁמַת כָּל־חַי וְגַם נַעֲרִיצָךְ ⋄	nishmat kol chai v'gam na-aritzach,
אֱכוֹל בְּשִׂמְחָה כִּי כְבָר רָצָךְ ⋄	echol b'simcha ki k'var ratzach.

שְׁמֵי שָׁמַיִם...　*Sh'mei shamayim eretz v'yamin...*

בְּמִשְׁנֶה לֶחֶם וְקִדּוּשׁ רַבָּא ⋄	B'mishneh lechem v'kidush raba,
בְּרֹב מַטְעַמִּים וְרוּחַ נְדִיבָה ⋄	b'rov mat'amim v'ruach n'diva,
יִזְכּוּ לְרַב טוּב הַמִּתְעַנְּגִים בָּהּ ⋄	yizku l'rav tuv mitan'gim ba,
בְּבִיאַת גּוֹאֵל לְעוֹלָם הַבָּא ⋄	b'viyat go-eil l'olam haba.

שְׁמֵי שָׁמַיִם...　*Sh'mei shamayim eretz v'yamin...*

To rest and rejoice a Jewish right,
This Shabbat day of sheer delight,
Those who keep it say this Friday night,
In six days God made the world with God's might.

The highest heavens, earth and sea,
The angels above, in majesty,
Monsters and man and beasts running free,
The strength of the worlds. Almighty is God.

This God declared to the people God chose:
Keep holy this day from its start to its close.
The Shabbat God loves like a jewel that glows,
This day God rested from work in repose.

For keeping the Shabbat, God strengthens you,
Pray and God will answer strong and true,
Say the Shabbat prayers as a loyal Jew,
Then eat with joy, for God likes what you do.

With two good loaves and Kiddush wine,
Delicious food for all to dine,
You earn for your joy a reward so fine,
When the Messiah will make a new world shine.

The acrostic gives the name *Moshe*. Beyond this,
the identity of the author is unknown.

מפי אל Mipi El

From God's mouth will Israel be blessed

מִפִּי אֵל, מִפִּי אֵל, יְבֹרַךְ יִשְׂרָאֵל.   Mipi Eil, mipi Eil y'vorach Yisrael.

אֵין אַדִּיר כַּיְיָ   Ein adir kadonai,

אֵין בָּרוּךְ כְּבֶן עַמְרָם   ein baruch k'ven Amram,

אֵין גְּדֻלָּה כַּתּוֹרָה   ein g'dulah katorah,

אֵין דּוֹרְשֶׁיהָ כְּיִשְׂרָאֵל   ein dorsheha k'Yisrael.

מִפִּי אֵל...   *Mipi Eil..*

אֵין הָדוּר כַּיְיָ   Ein hadur kadonai,

אֵין וָתִיק כְּבֶן עַמְרָם   ein vatik k'ven Amram,

אֵין זְכִיָּה כַּתּוֹרָה   ein z'chi-ya kaTorah,

אֵין חֲכָמֶיהָ כְּיִשְׂרָאֵל   ein chachameha k'Yisrael.

מִפִּי אֵל...   *Mipi Eil...*

אֵין טָהוֹר כַּיְיָ   Ein tahor kadonai,

אֵין יָשָׁר כְּבֶן עַמְרָם   ein yashar k'ven Amram,

אֵין כְּבֻדָּה כַּתּוֹרָה   ein k'vuda kaTorah,

אֵין לוֹמְדֶיהָ כְּיִשְׂרָאֵל   ein lomdeha k'Yisrael.

מִפִּי אֵל...   *Mipi Eil...*

אֵין מֶלֶךְ כַּיְיָ   Ein melech kadonai,

אֵין נָבִיא כְּבֶן עַמְרָם   ein navi k'ven Amram,

אֵין סְגֻלָּה כַּתּוֹרָה   ein s'gula kaTorah,

אֵין עוֹסְקֶיהָ כְּיִשְׂרָאֵל   ein os'keha k'Yisrael

מִפִּי אֵל...   *Mipi Eil...*

אֵין פּוֹדֶה כַּיְיָ   Ein podeh kadonai,

אֵין צַדִּיק כְּבֶן עַמְרָם   ein tzadik k'ven Amram,

אֵין קְדֻשָּׁה כַּתּוֹרָה   ein k'dusha kaTorah,

אֵין רוֹמְמֶיהָ כְּיִשְׂרָאֵל   ein rom'meha k'Yisrael.

מִפִּי אֵל...   *Mipi Eil...*

34

אֵין קָדוֹשׁ כַּיי ∘
אֵין רַחוּם כְּבֶן עַמְרָם ∘
אֵין שְׁמִירָה כַּתּוֹרָה ∘
אֵין תּוֹמְכֶיהָ כְּיִשְׂרָאֵל ∘
מִפִּי אֵל...

Ein kadosh kadonai,
ein rachum k'ven Amram,
ein sh'mira kaTorah,
ein tom'cheha k'Yisrael.

Mipi Eil...

God will bless Israel.

There is no other as powerful as God, and none as blessed as Moses, the son of Amram. There is no other as great as the Torah, and those who profess, as Israel.

God will bless Israel.

There is no better adornment such as God, and no better friend than Moses, the son of Amram. There is no possession like the Torah, and those who study, as Israel.

God will bless Israel.

There is no other as pure as God, and none as straightforward as Moses, the son of Amram. There is no honor like the Torah, and no students, as Israel.

God will bless Israel.

There is no king like God, and no prophet like Moses, the son of Amram. There is no treasure as the Torah, and no possessions as Israel.

God will bless Israel.

There is no redeemer as God, and no one as righteous as Moses, the son of Amram. There is nothing as blessed as the Torah, and nothing as majestic as Israel.

God will bless Israel.

There is nothing as holy as God, and none so merciful as Moses, the son of Amram. There is no guard as the Torah, and no supporter like Israel.

God will bless Israel.

An alphabetical acrostic from the liturgy.

35

צוּר מִשֶּׁלוֹ *Tzur Mishelo*

Gratitude to God for providing for our nourishment

צוּר מִשֶּׁלוֹ אָכַלְנוּ בָּרְכוּ אֱמוּנַי	Tzur, mishelo achalnu bar'chu emunai;
שָׂבַעְנוּ וְהוֹתַרְנוּ כִּדְבַר יי	savanu v'hotarnu kidvar Adonai.
הַזָּן אֶת עוֹלָמוֹ רוֹעֵנוּ אָבִינוּ	Hazan et olamo, ro-einu avinu,
אָכַלְנוּ אֶת לַחְמוֹ וְיֵינוֹ שָׁתִינוּ	achalnu et lachmo, v'yeino shatinu,
עַל כֵּן נוֹדֶה לִשְׁמוֹ	al kein nodeh lishmo
וּנְהַלְּלוֹ בְּפִינוּ	un-hal'lo b'finu,
אָמַרְנוּ וְעָנֵינוּ אֵין קָדוֹשׁ כַּיי	amarnu v'aninu ein kadosh kadonai.
צוּר מִשֶּׁלוֹ...	*Tzur mishelo...*
בְּשִׁיר וְקוֹל תּוֹדָה	B'shir v'kol todah,
נְבָרֵךְ אֱלֹהֵינוּ	n'vareich Eloheinu,
עַל אֶרֶץ חֶמְדָּה	al eretz chemda,
שֶׁהִנְחִיל לַאֲבוֹתֵינוּ	shehinchil la-avoteinu,
מָזוֹן וְצֵדָה	mazon v'tzeida,
הִשְׂבִּיעַ לְנַפְשֵׁנוּ	hisbia l'nafsheinu,
חַסְדּוֹ גָּבַר עָלֵינוּ	chasdo gavar aleinu,
וֶאֱמֶת יי.	ve-emet Adonai.
צוּר מִשֶּׁלוֹ...	*Tzur mishelo...*
רַחֵם בְּחַסְדֶּךָ	Racheim b'chasdecha
עַל עַמְּךָ צוּרֵנוּ	al amcha tzureinu,
עַל צִיּוֹן מִשְׁכַּן כְּבוֹדֶךָ	al tzion mishkan k'vodecha
זְבוּל בֵּית תִּפְאַרְתֵּנוּ	z'vul beit tifarteinu.
בֶּן דָּוִד עַבְדֶּךָ	Ben David avdecha
יָבוֹא וְיִגְאָלֵנוּ	yavo v'yig-aleinu,
רוּחַ אַפֵּינוּ מְשִׁיחַ יי	ruach apeinu Meshiach Adonai.
צוּר מִשֶּׁלוֹ...	*Tzur mishelo...*

יִבָּנֶה הַמִּקְדָּשׁ	Yibaneh hamikdash
עִיר צִיּוֹן תְּמַלֵּא	ir Tzion t'malei,
וְשָׁם נָשִׁיר שִׁיר חָדָשׁ	v'sham nashir shir chadash
וּבִרְנָנָה נַעֲלֶה	u-virnana na-aleh,
הָרַחֲמָן הַנִּקְדָּשׁ	Harachaman hanikdash
יִתְבָּרַךְ וְיִתְעַלֶּה	yitbarach v'yitaleh,
עַל כּוֹס יַיִן מָלֵא	al kos yayin malei
כְּבִרְכַּת יי	k'virkat Adonai.
צוּר מִשֶּׁלּוֹ...	*Tzur mishelo...*

We've eaten God's food; let's adore and bless God in one accord;
We've had enough and more, by the word of the Lord.

God keeps God's world well fed, this Shepherd, Parent of mine.
We ate God's tasty bread and drank God's goodly wine;
Let's thank God, feeling glad, and praise God as we dine,
Singing as we recline: None is holy like the Lord.
  We've eaten God's food...

Our song of thanks we sound to bless the God we know,
God gave a wondrous land to our ancestors long ago;
With food by God's command God satisfies us so,
God's love for us will flow, for true is God, our Lord.
  We've eaten God's food...

Have mercy, Lord: O pity the people in Your care,
And Zion Your holy city, the place of Your Temple so fair;
O let Messiah not wait, he must rescue us from despair,
Our very breath and air is this chosen man of the Lord,
  We've eaten God's food...

Rebuild Your Temple again, let Zion be full as before,
We'll sing a new song then, go up with praise as of yore,
The Merciful, Holy One we'll bless now and adore,
So fill the cup once more, by the blessing of the Lord.
  We've eaten God's food...

Author unknown

37

יָהּ רִבּוֹן Yah Ribon

God as Master, eternal ruler of everything

יָהּ רִבּוֹן עָלַם וְעָלְמַיָּא	Yah ribon alam v'almaya,
אַנְתְּ הוּא מַלְכָּא מֶלֶךְ מַלְכַיָּא	ant hu malka melech malchaya,
עוֹבַד גְּבוּרְתֵּךְ וְתִמְהַיָּא	ovad g'vurteich v'timhaya,
שְׁפַר קֳדָמָךְ לְהַחֲוָיָא	sh'far kodamach l'hachavaya.

יָהּ רִבּוֹן עָלַם...   *Yah ribon alam...*

שְׁבָחִין אֲסַדֵּר צַפְרָא וְרַמְשָׁא	Sh'vachin asader tzafra v'ramsha,
לָךְ אֱלָהָא קַדִּישָׁא דִּי בְרָא	lach elaha kadisha di v'ra
כָּל נַפְשָׁא	chol nafsha,
עִירִין קַדִּישִׁין וּבְנֵי אֱנָשָׁא	irin kadishin uv'nei enasha,
חֵיוַת בָּרָא וְעוֹפֵי שְׁמַיָּא	cheivat bara v'ofei sh'maya.

יָהּ רִבּוֹן עָלַם...   *Yah ribon alam...*

רַבְרְבִין עוֹבְדָיךְ וְתַקִּיפִין	Ravr'vin ovdayich v'takifin,
מָכֵךְ רְמַיָּא וְזָקֵיף כְּפִיפִין	macheich r'maya v'zakeif k'fifin,
לוּ יִחְיֶה גְּבַר שְׁנִין אַלְפִין	lu y'chei g'var sh'nin alfin,
לָא יֵעוֹל גְּבוּרְתֵּךְ בְּחֻשְׁבְּנַיָּא	la yei-ol g'vurteich b'chushb'naya.

יָהּ רִבּוֹן עָלַם...   *Yah ribon alam...*

אֱלָהָא דִּי לֵהּ יְקָר וּרְבוּתָא	Elaha di lei y'kar ur'vuta,
פְּרוֹק יָת עָנָךְ מִפּוּם אַרְיָוָתָא	p'rok yat anach mipum aryavata,
וְאַפֵּיק יָת עַמֵּךְ מִגּוֹ גָלוּתָא	v'apeik yat amach migo galuta,
עַמֵּךְ דִּי בְחַרְתְּ מִכָּל אֻמַּיָּא	amech di v'chart mikol umaya.

יָהּ רִבּוֹן עָלַם...   *Yah ribon alam...*

לְמִקְדָּשֵׁךְ תּוּב וּלְקֹדֶשׁ קֻדְשִׁין	L'mikdashech tuv ul-kodesh kudshin,
אֲתַר דִּי בֵהּ יֶחֱדוּן רוּחִין וְנַפְשִׁין	atar di vei yechedun ruchin v'nafshin,
וִיזַמְּרוּן לָךְ שִׁירִין וְרַחֲשִׁין	vizamrun lach shirin v'rachashin,
בִּירוּשְׁלֵם קַרְתָּא דְשׁוּפְרַיָּא	birush-leim karta d'shufraya

יָהּ רִבּוֹן עָלַם...   *Yah ribon alam...*

Almighty Master of worlds, of everything,
You are the Sovereign who rules every king,
Your wonders and deeds leave us marvelling,
It would be good to sing Your glory.
Morning and evening I'll sing Your worth,
For with You, holy God, we all had birth,
Spirits in heaven and people on earth,
Beasts in the field and birds on the wing.
Your deeds are mighty for strong and weak,
You humble the proud and honor the meek,
If a thousand years I could live and speak,
I could not reveal all the wonders You bring.
Dear God, to whom all glory goes,
O save Your flock from Lion-like foes,
Set free Your people from exile's woes,
Of all nations You chose us; to You we cling,
Return to Your Temple, Your holiest place,
Where spirits and souls will rejoice in Your grace,
And sing to Your glory with shining face,
In Your city, Jerusalem, as lovely as spring.

By Israel ben Moses Najara

יוֹם שַׁבָּתוֹן *Yom Shabbaton*

We recall receiving the Ten Commandments joyously
and ask for strength through Shabbat rest.

יוֹם שַׁבָּתוֹן אֵין לִשְׁכֹּחַ	Yom Shabbaton ein lishko-ach,
זִכְרוֹ כְּרֵיחַ הַנִּיחֹחַ	zichro k'rei-ach hanicho-ach,
יוֹנָה מָצְאָה בוֹ מָנוֹחַ	yona matz'a vo mano-ach,
וְשָׁם יָנוּחוּ יְגִיעֵי כֹחַ	v'sham yanuchu y'gi-ei choach.
יוֹנָה מָצְאָה....	*Yona matz'a...*
הַיּוֹם נִכְבָּד לִבְנֵי אֱמוּנִים	Hayom nichbad livnei emunim,
זְהִירִים לְשָׁמְרוֹ אָבוֹת וּבָנִים	z'hirim l'shomro avot u'vanim,
חָקוּק בִּשְׁנֵי לֻחוֹת אֲבָנִים	chakuk bishnei luchot avanim,
מֵרֹב אוֹנִים וְאַמִּיץ כֹּחַ	meirov onim v'amitz ko-ach.
יוֹנָה מָצְאָה....	*Yona matz'a...*
וּבָאוּ כֻלָּם בִּבְרִית יַחַד	Uva-u chulam biv'rit yachad,
נַעֲשֶׂה וְנִשְׁמַע אָמְרוּ כְּאֶחָד	na-aseh v'nishma amru k'echad,
וּפָתְחוּ וְעָנוּ יְיָ אֶחָד	ufat-chu v'anu Adonai echad,
בָּרוּךְ הַנּוֹתֵן לַיָּעֵף כֹּחַ	baruch hanotein laya-eif ko-ach.
יוֹנָה מָצְאָה....	*Yona matz'a...*
דִּבֶּר בְּקָדְשׁוֹ בְּהַר הַמֹּר	Diber b'kodsho b'har hamor,
יוֹם הַשְּׁבִיעִי זָכוֹר וְשָׁמוֹר	yom hashvi-i zachor v'shamor,
וְכָל־פִּקּוּדָיו יַחַד לִגְמֹר	v'chol pikudav yachad ligmor,
חַזֵּק מָתְנַיִם וְאַמֵּץ כֹּחַ	chazeik motnayim v'ameitz koach.
יוֹנָה מָצְאָה....	*Yona matz'a...*
הָעָם אֲשֶׁר נָע כַּצֹּאן תָּעָה	Ha'am asher na katzon ta-a,
יִזְכּוֹר לְפָקְדוֹ בְּרִית וּשְׁבוּעָה	yizkor l'fokdo brit ush'vua,
לְבַל יַעֲבָר־בָּם מִקְרֵה רָעָה	l'val ya-avor bam mikrei ra-a,
כַּאֲשֶׁר נִשְׁבַּע עַל מֵי נֹחַ	ka-asher nishba al mei no-ach.
יוֹנָה מָצְאָה....	*Yona matz'a...*

40

Unforgettable Shabbat, beyond compare,
Its memory sweet as a fragrance rare.
As a dove our people find rest from care,
The weary repose, its joys to share.
    As a dove...

A faithful people honor this day,
Parents and children take care to obey,
For so do the Ten Commandments say.
In the tablets of stone God wrote it there.
    As a dove...

At Sinai our people stood and swore,
"We'll do it, we'll listen!" came their roar.
"The Lord is One," said they, and more
"Giving strength to the weary, joy in despair."
    As a dove...

At Sinai God spoke clear as a bell,
"Keep holy the Shabbat, remember it well,
Learn all its rules wherever you dwell,
Grow strong in rest, your strength repair."
    As a dove...

We wander in Exile like straying sheep,
Remember our oath, the Shabbat to keep,
Let evil not touch us in rest or sleep,
As long ago You once did swear.
    As a dove...

The acrostic spells the name *Yehuda*.
This composition has been attributed to
Yehudah Halevi.

יוֹם זֶה מְכֻבָּד   *Yom Zeh M'Chubad*

Give honor to Shabbat through its observance

יוֹם זֶה מְכֻבָּד מִכָּל־יָמִים
כִּי בוֹ שָׁבַת צוּר עוֹלָמִים

Yom zeh m'chubad mikol yamim,
ki vo shavat tzur olamim.

שֵׁשֶׁת יָמִים תַּעֲשֶׂה מְלַאכְתֶּךָ
וְיוֹם הַשְּׁבִיעִי לֵאלֹהֶיךָ
שַׁבָּת לֹא תַעֲשֶׂה בוֹ מְלָאכָה
כִּי כֹל עָשָׂה שֵׁשֶׁת יָמִים
יוֹם זֶה מְכֻבָּד מִכָּל־יָמִים...

Sheishet yamim asei m'lachtecha,
v'yom hashvi-I leilohecha,
Shabbat lo ta-aseh vo m'lacha
ki chol asa sheishet yamim.
Yom zeh m'chubad mi kol yamim...

רִאשׁוֹן הוּא לְמִקְרָאֵי קֹדֶשׁ
יוֹם שַׁבָּתוֹן יוֹם שַׁבַּת קֹדֶשׁ
עַל כֵּן כָּל־אִישׁ בְּיֵינוֹ יְקַדֵּשׁ
עַל שְׁתֵּי לֶחֶם יִבְצְעוּ תְמִימִים
יוֹם זֶה מְכֻבָּד מִכָּל־יָמִים...

Rishon hu l'mikra-ei kodesh,
yom Shabbaton yom Shabbat kodesh,
al kein kol ish b'yeino y'kadeish,
al shtei lechem yivtz'u t'mimim.
Yom zeh m'chubad mi kol yamim...

אֱכֹל מַשְׁמַנִּים שְׁתֵה מַמְתַּקִּים
כִּי אֵל יִתֵּן לְכָל בּוֹ דְבֵקִים
בֶּגֶד לִלְבֹּשׁ לֶחֶם חֻקִּים
בָּשָׂר וְדָגִים וְכָל־מַטְעַמִּים
יוֹם זֶה מְכֻבָּד מִכָּל־יָמִים...

Echol mashmanim shtei mamtakim,
ki Eil yitein l'chol bo d'veikim,
beged lilbosh lechem chukim,
basar v'dagim v'chol matamim.
Yom zeh m'chubad mi kol yamim...

לֹא תֶחְסַר כֹּל בּוֹ וְאָכַלְתָּ
וְשָׂבַעְתָּ וּבֵרַכְתָּ
אֶת־יי אֱלֹהֶיךָ אֲשֶׁר אָהַבְתָּ
כִּי בֵרַכְךָ מִכָּל־הָעַמִּים
יוֹם זֶה מְכֻבָּד מִכָּל־יָמִים...

Lo techsar kol bo v'achalta,
v'savata uveirachta
et Adonai Elohecha asher ahavta,
ki veirach'cha mikol ha-amim
Yom zeh m'chubad mi kol yamim...

הַשָּׁמַיִם מְסַפְּרִים כְּבוֹדוֹ ❖
וְגַם־הָאָרֶץ מָלְאָה חַסְדּוֹ ❖
רְאוּ כִּי כָל־אֵלֶּה עָשְׂתָה יָדוֹ ❖
כִּי הוּא הַצּוּר פָּעֳלוֹ תָמִים ❖
יוֹם זֶה מְכֻבָּד מִכָּל־יָמִים...

Hashamayim m'saprim k'vodo,
v'gam ha-aretz mal-a chasdo,
r'u ki chol cileh asta yado,
ki hu hatzur pa-olo tamim.
Yom zeh m'chubad mi kol yamim...

This day is honored, above all blessed,
This day the God of the worlds did rest.
You have six days to labor away
The seventh is God's, God's special day.
No work on the Shabbat, O this obey,
For in six God made all, by God's behest.
This day is honored...

The first of the holy days is this,
A Shabbat of rest and holy bless.
Then Kiddush on wine don't ever miss,
To bless God over two loaves is best.
This day is honored...

Eat tasty food, drink well and sing,
For God provides, if to God you cling,
Clothing and food so nourishing,
Good meat and fish to eat with zest.
This day is honored...

You'll lack for nothing, you'll eat with cheer,
So dine and wine and singing clear,
Bless the Lord and love and revere,
For above all did God bless in your nest.
This day is honored...

God's glory is told by the heavens above,
The earth is filled with God's kindness and love,
See: God made all, to the gentlest dove,
God's work is perfect, east or west.
This day is honored...

The acrostic gives the name *Yisrael*. Otherwise,
the identity of the author is unknown.

43

The mood at S'udah Shlishit is a subdued one. Our Shabbat joy is dimmed by the thought that the Shabbat will be leaving us soon. The songs at S'udah Shlishit reflect this mood and the melodies are quiet and peaceful.

Additional songs for S'udah Shlishit can be found in the *Shirim K'tzarim* (Short Songs) section.

מזמור לדוד / *Mizmor L'David*

מִזְמוֹר לְדָוִד, יי רֹעִי לֹא
אֶחְסָר. בִּנְאוֹת דֶּשֶׁא יַרְבִּיצֵנִי,
עַל־מֵי מְנֻחוֹת יְנַהֲלֵנִי. נַפְשִׁי
יְשׁוֹבֵב, יַנְחֵנִי בְמַעְגְּלֵי־צֶדֶק
לְמַעַן שְׁמוֹ. גַּם כִּי־אֵלֵךְ
בְּגֵיא צַלְמָוֶת לֹא־אִירָא
רָע כִּי־אַתָּה עִמָּדִי שִׁבְטְךָ
וּמִשְׁעַנְתֶּךָ הֵמָּה יְנַחֲמֻנִי.
תַּעֲרֹךְ לְפָנַי | שֻׁלְחָן נֶגֶד
צֹרְרָי דִּשַּׁנְתָּ בַשֶּׁמֶן רֹאשִׁי
כּוֹסִי רְוָיָה. אַךְ טוֹב וָחֶסֶד
יִרְדְּפוּנִי כָּל־יְמֵי חַיָּי, וְשַׁבְתִּי
בְּבֵית יי לְאֹרֶךְ יָמִים.

תהילים כג

Mizmor l'David, Adonai ro-i lo
echsar. Binot desheh yarbitzeini,
al mei m'nuchot y'nahaleini. Nafshi
y'shoveiv, yancheini b'maglei tzedek
l'ma-an sh'mo. Gam ki eileich
b'gei tzalmavet lo ira,
ra ki ata imadi, shivt'cha
u-mishantecha heima y'nachamuni.
Ta-aroch l'fanai shulchan neged
tzor'rai, dishanta vashemen roshi
kosi r'vaya. Ach tov vachesed
yird'funi kol y'mei chayai, v'shavti
b'veit Adonai l'orech yamim.

Psalms 23

The Lord is my shepherd, I shall not want. God gives me repose in green meadows. God leads me beside the still waters; God revives my spirit. God guides me on the right path, for that is God's nature. Though I walk in the valley of the shadow of death, I fear no harm, for You are with me. Your staff and Your rod comfort me. You prepare a banquet for me in the presence of my foes. You anoint my head with oil; my cup overflows. Surely goodness and kindness shall be my portion all the days of my life. And I shall dwell in the House of the Lord forever.

From *The Bond of Life*, edited by Rabbi Jules Harlow. Copyright ©1975, 1983 by The Rabbinical Assembly. Reprinted by permission of Rabbinical Assembly.

ידיד נפש   *Y'did Nefesh*

God as the soul mate of the Jewish people

יְדִיד נֶפֶשׁ, אָב הָרַחֲמָן,	Y'did nefesh, av harachaman,
מְשׁוֹךְ עַבְדָּךְ אֶל רְצוֹנָךְ,	m'shoch avdach Eil r'tzonach,
יָרוּץ עַבְדָּךְ כְּמוֹ אַיָּל,	ya-rutz avdach k'mo ayal,
יִשְׁתַּחֲוֶה אֶל מוּל הֲדָרָךְ,	yishta-chaveh Eil mul hadarach,
יֶעֱרַב לוֹ יְדִידוּתָךְ,	ye-erav lo y'didutach,
מִנֹּפֶת צוּף וְכָל־טָעַם.	minofet tzuf v'chol ta-am.

הָדוּר נָאֶה, זִיו הָעוֹלָם,	Hadur na-eh ziv ha-olam,
נַפְשִׁי חוֹלַת אַהֲבָתָךְ,	nafshi cholat ahavatach,
אָנָּא, אֵל נָא, רְפָא נָא לָהּ,	ana, Eil na, r'fa na la,
בְּהַרְאוֹת לָהּ נֹעַם זִיוָךְ,	b'har'ot la noam zivach,
אָז תִּתְחַזֵּק וְתִתְרַפֵּא,	az titchazeik v'titrapei,
וְהָיְתָה לָךְ שִׁפְחַת עוֹלָם.	v'haita lach shif-chat olam.

וָתִיק, יֶהֱמוּ רַחֲמֶיךָ,	Vatik yehemu rachamecha,
וְחוּס נָא עַל בֵּן אוֹהֲבָךְ,	v'chus na al bein ohavach,
כִּי זֶה כַּמָּה נִכְסוֹף נִכְסַף,	ki ze kama nichsof nichsaf,
לִרְאוֹת בְּתִפְאֶרֶת עֻזָּךְ,	lirot b'tiferet u-zach,
אָנָּא, אֵלִי, מַחְמַד לִבִּי,	ana Eili machmad libi,
חוּשָׁה נָא וְאַל תִּתְעַלָּם.	chusha na v'al titalam.

הִגָּלֵה נָא וּפְרוֹשׂ, חָבִיב עָלַי,	Higaleh na uf'ros chaviv alai,
אֶת־סֻכַּת שְׁלוֹמָךְ,	et sukat sh'lomach,
תָּאִיר אֶרֶץ מִכְּבוֹדָךְ,	ta-ir eretz mikvodach,
נָגִילָה וְנִשְׂמְחָה בָּךְ,	nagila v'nis'm'cha bach,
מַהֵר, אָהוּב, כִּי בָא מוֹעֵד,	maheir, ahuv, ki va mo-eid,
וְחָנֵּנִי כִּימֵי עוֹלָם.	v'chonelni kimei olam.

אלעזר אזיקרי

A *piyyut* written by 16th century Kabbalist, Elazar Azikri

45

Soul mate, loving God, compassion's gentle source,
Take my disposition and shape it to Your will.
Like a darting deer will I rush to You.
Before your glorious presence humbly will I bow.
Let Your sweet love delight me with its thrill,
Because no other dainty will my still.

How splendid is Your light, illumining the world.
My soul is weary yearning for Your love's delight.
Please, good God, do heal her; reveal to her Your face,
The pleasure of Your presence, bathed in Your grace.
She will find strength and healing in Your sight;
Forever will she serve You, grateful, with all her might.

What mercy stirs in You since days of old, my God.
Be kind to me, Your own child; my love for You requite.
With deep and endless longing I yearned for Your embrace,
To see my light in Your light, basking in Your grace.
My heart's desire, find me worthy in Your sight.
Do not delay Your mercy, please hide not Your light.

Reveal Yourself, Beloved, for all the world to see,
And shelter me in peace beneath Your canopy.
Illumine all creation, lighting up the earth,
And we shall celebrate You in choruses of mirth.
The time, my Love, is now; rush, be quick, be bold.
Let Your favor grace me, in the spirit of days of old.

ברכת המזון BIRKAT HAMAZON
GRACE AFTER MEALS

לשבת ויום טוב

שִׁיר הַמַּעֲלוֹת, בְּשׁוּב יי
אֶת־שִׁיבַת צִיּוֹן הָיִינוּ כְּחֹלְמִים.
אָז יִמָּלֵא שְׂחוֹק פִּינוּ וּלְשׁוֹנֵנוּ
רִנָּה, אָז יֹאמְרוּ בַגּוֹיִם, הִגְדִּיל
יי לַעֲשׂוֹת עִם־אֵלֶּה. הִגְדִּיל
יי לַעֲשׂוֹת עִמָּנוּ, הָיִינוּ
שְׂמֵחִים. שׁוּבָה יי אֶת־
שְׁבִיתֵנוּ כַּאֲפִיקִים בַּנֶּגֶב.
הַזֹּרְעִים בְּדִמְעָה בְּרִנָּה יִקְצֹרוּ.
הָלוֹךְ יֵלֵךְ וּבָכֹה, נֹשֵׂא
מֶשֶׁךְ הַזָּרַע, בֹּא יָבֹא
בְרִנָּה נֹשֵׂא אֲלֻמֹּתָיו.

תהילים קכו

For Shabbat and Festivals:

Shir Hama-a-lot, b'shuv Adonai
et shivat Tzion haylnu k'cholmim,
az y'malei s'chok pinu ul-shoneinu
rina, az yomru vagoyim: higdil
Adonai la-a-sot im eileh. Higdil
Adonai la-a-sot imanu, hayinu
s'meichim. Shuva Adonai et
sh'viteinu ka-afikim banegev.
Hazor'im b'dima b'rina yik-tzoru,
haloch yeileich uvacho, nosei
meshech hazara. Bo yavo
v'rina nosei alumotav.

Psalms 126

Some people add:

תְּהִלַּת יי יְדַבֶּר פִּי, וִיבָרֵךְ
כָּל־בָּשָׂר שֵׁם קָדְשׁוֹ לְעוֹלָם
וָעֶד. וַאֲנַחְנוּ נְבָרֵךְ יָהּ
מֵעַתָּה וְעַד־עוֹלָם, הַלְלוּיָהּ.
הוֹדוּ לַיי כִּי־טוֹב, כִּי לְעוֹלָם
חַסְדּוֹ. מִי יְמַלֵּל גְּבוּרוֹת יי,
יַשְׁמִיעַ, כָּל־תְּהִלָּתוֹ.

תהילים קמה:כא, קטו:יח, קיח:א, קו:ב

T'hilat Adonai y'daber pi vivareich
kol basar sheim kodsho l'olam
va-ed. Va-anachnu n'vareich ya
mei-ata v'ad olam halleluyah.
Hodu Ladonai ki tov ki l'olam
chasdo. Mi y'maleil g'vurot Adonai
yashmi-a kol t'hilato.

Psalms 145:21, 115:18, 118:1, 106:2

47

A Song of Ascent. When the Lord brought the exiles back to Zion
We were like dreamers.
Then were our mouths filled with laughter
and our tongues with ringing song.
Then was it said among the nations:
"The Lord has done great things for them."
The Lord has done great things for us.
And we rejoiced.
Bring us from exile, Lord, as the streams return to the Negev;
Then they who sow in tears shall reap in joy.
Though one weeps as he scatters the measure of seed,
He shall return home with joy, bearing his sheaves.

Some people add:

Now let my mouth declare the Lord's praise, and let the whole human race bless God's holy name for all time. As for us, we will bless the Lord from now on and forever more: praise the Lord! Give thanks to the Lord for God is good, for God's kindness is everlasting! Who can describe the mighty deeds of the Lord, or utter all God's praise?

When three or more have eaten together:
(Words in parentheses are recited only when there is a minyan present).

Leader:

חֲבֵרֵי נְבָרֵךְ   Chaverei n'vareich

Friends, let us thank God.

Group recites, and leader repeats:

יְהִי שֵׁם יי מְבֹרָךְ   Y'hi sheim Adonai m'vorach
מֵעַתָּה וְעַד עוֹלָם.   mei-atah v'ad olam.

Blessed is the name of the Lord from now and forever.

Leader:

בִּרְשׁוּת חֲבֵרַי, נְבָרֵךְ   Birshut chave'rei, n'vareich
(אֱלֹהֵינוּ) שֶׁאָכַלְנוּ מִשֶּׁלוֹ.   (Eloheinu) she-achalnu mishelo.

With your permission, let us thank God (let us thank our God)
whose food we have eaten.

Group recites, and leader repeats:

בָּרוּךְ (אֱלֹהֵינוּ) שֶׁאָכַלְנוּ   Baruch (Eloheinu) she-achalnu
מִשֶּׁלוֹ וּבְטוּבוֹ חָיִינוּ.   mishelo u'vtuvo chayinu

Blessed is God (Blessed is our God) whose food we have
eaten and through whose goodness we live.

All:

בָּרוּךְ הוּא וּבָרוּךְ שְׁמוֹ:   Baruch hu u-varuch sh'mo:

Blessed is God and blessed is God's name:

When fewer than three have eaten together, Birkat Hamazon *begins here:*

בָּרוּךְ אַתָּה יי אֱלֹהֵינוּ מֶלֶךְ
הָעוֹלָם, הַזָּן אֶת־הָעוֹלָם כֻּלּוֹ
בְּטוּבוֹ בְּחֵן בְּחֶסֶד וּבְרַחֲמִים.
הוּא נוֹתֵן לֶחֶם לְכָל־בָּשָׂר, כִּי
לְעוֹלָם חַסְדּוֹ. וּבְטוּבוֹ הַגָּדוֹל
תָּמִיד לֹא חָסַר לָנוּ, וְאַל
יֶחְסַר־לָנוּ מָזוֹן לְעוֹלָם וָעֶד.
בַּעֲבוּר שְׁמוֹ הַגָּדוֹל, כִּי הוּא
אֵל זָן וּמְפַרְנֵס לַכֹּל וּמֵטִיב
לַכֹּל, וּמֵכִין מָזוֹן לְכָל־בְּרִיּוֹתָיו
אֲשֶׁר בָּרָא. בָּרוּךְ אַתָּה יי,
הַזָּן אֶת־הַכֹּל.

Baruch atah Adonai Eloheinu melech
ha-olam, zan et ha-olam kulo
b'tuvo b'chein b'chesed uv-rachamim.
Hu notein lechem l'chol basar, ki
l'olam chasdo. Uv-tuvo hagadol
tamid lo chasar lanu v'al
yechsar lanu mazon l'olam va-ed.
Ba-avur sh'mo hagadol, ki hu
el zan um-farneis lakol, u-meitiv
lakol u-meichin mazon l'chol b'riyotav
asher bara. Baruch atah Adonai,
zan et hakol.

Blessed is the Lord our God, Sovereign of the universe, who sustains the entire world with goodness, kindness and mercy. God gives food to all creatures, for God's mercy is everlasting. Through God's abundant goodness we have never yet been in want; may we never be in want of sustenance for the sake of God's great name. God sustains all, does good to all, and provides food for all the creatures whom God has created. Blessed is the Lord, who provides food for all.

נוֹדֶה לְךָ, יי אֱלֹהֵינוּ, עַל
שֶׁהִנְחַלְתָּ לַאֲבוֹתֵינוּ אֶרֶץ
חֶמְדָּה טוֹבָה וּרְחָבָה, וְעַל
שֶׁהוֹצֵאתָנוּ, יי אֱלֹהֵינוּ,
מֵאֶרֶץ מִצְרַיִם, וּפְדִיתָנוּ מִבֵּית
עֲבָדִים, וְעַל בְּרִיתְךָ שֶׁחָתַמְתָּ
בִּבְשָׂרֵנוּ, וְעַל תּוֹרָתְךָ
שֶׁלִּמַּדְתָּנוּ, וְעַל חֻקֶּיךָ
שֶׁהוֹדַעְתָּנוּ, וְעַל חַיִּים חֵן

Nodeh l'cha, Adonai Eloheinu, al
she-hinchalta la-avoteinu eretz
chemda tovah ur-chava, v'al
she-hotzeitanu Adonai Eloheinu
mei-eretz mitzrayim uf-ditanu mibeit
avadim, v'al brit'cha she-chatamta
biv-sareinu, v'al torat-cha
she-limad-tanu, v'al chukecha
she-hodatanu, v'al chayim chein

וָחֶסֶד שֶׁחוֹנַנְתָּנוּ, וְעַל
אֲכִילַת מָזוֹן שָׁאַתָּה זָן וּמְפַרְנֵס
אוֹתָנוּ תָּמִיד, בְּכָל־יוֹם
וּבְכָל־עֵת וּבְכָל־שָׁעָה.

va-chesed she-chonantanu, v'al
achilat mazon she-ata zan umfarneis
otanu tamid, b'chol yom
uv-chol eit uv-chol sha'ah.

We thank the Lord our God for having given a lovely and spacious land to our ancestors as a heritage; for having liberated us from the land of Egypt and freed us from the house of bondage; for the covenant which God has sealed in our flesh; for the Torah which God has taught us, for the laws which God has made known to us; for the life, grace and lovingkindness which God has bestowed upon us, and for the sustenance with which God nourishes and maintains us continually, in every season, every day, even every hour.

On Chanukkah, Purim, and Yom Ha'atzmaut add:

עַל הַנִּסִּים וְעַל הַפֻּרְקָן, וְעַל
הַגְּבוּרוֹת, וְעַל הַתְּשׁוּעוֹת, וְעַל
הַמִּלְחָמוֹת שֶׁעָשִׂיתָ לַאֲבוֹתֵינוּ
בַּיָּמִים הָהֵם בַּזְּמַן הַזֶּה.

Al hanisim v'al hapurkan v'al
hag'vurot v'al hat'shuot, v'al
hamilchamot she-asita la-avoteinu
bayamim haheim bazman hazeh.

We thank God for the miracles, the deliverance, the mighty acts and the triumphant victories which God wrought for our ancestors in ancient days at this time of year.

בחנוכה: *On Chanukkah:*

בִּימֵי מַתִּתְיָהוּ בֶּן־יוֹחָנָן
כֹּהֵן גָּדוֹל, חַשְׁמוֹנַי וּבָנָיו,
כְּשֶׁעָמְדָה מַלְכוּת יָוָן
הָרְשָׁעָה עַל עַמְּךָ יִשְׂרָאֵל
לְהַשְׁכִּיחָם תּוֹרָתֶךָ
וּלְהַעֲבִירָם מֵחֻקֵּי רְצוֹנֶךָ,
וְאַתָּה בְּרַחֲמֶיךָ הָרַבִּים
עָמַדְתָּ לָהֶם בְּעֵת צָרָתָם,
רַבְתָּ אֶת־רִיבָם, דַּנְתָּ אֶת

Bimei Matityahu ben Yochanan
kohein gadol chashmonai u-vanav,
k'she-amda malchut yavan
har'sha'a' al amcha Yisrael
l'hash-kicham toratecha
ul-ha-aviram meichukei r'tzonecha,
v'ata b'rachamecha harabim
amad-ta lahem b'eit tzaratam,
ravta et rivam, danta et

51

דִּינָם, נָקַמְתָּ אֶת־נִקְמָתָם, dinam, nakamta et nikmatam,
מָסַרְתָּ גִבּוֹרִים בְּיַד חַלָּשִׁים masarta giborim b'yad chalashim
וְרַבִּים בְּיַד מְעַטִּים, וּטְמֵאִים v'rabim b'yad m'atim, ut-mei-im
בְּיַד טְהוֹרִים, וּרְשָׁעִים בְּיַד b'yad t'horim, ur-sha-im b'yad
צַדִּיקִים, וְזֵדִים בְּיַד עוֹסְקֵי tzadikim v'zeidim b'yad os'kei
תוֹרָתֶךָ. וּלְךָ עָשִׂיתָ שֵׁם גָּדוֹל toratecha. Ul-cha asita sheim gadol
וְקָדוֹשׁ בְּעוֹלָמֶךָ, וּלְעַמְּךָ v'kadosh b'olamecha, ul-amcha
יִשְׂרָאֵל עָשִׂיתָ תְּשׁוּעָה גְדוֹלָה Yisrael asita t'shu-a g'dola
וּפֻרְקָן כְּהַיּוֹם הַזֶּה. וְאַחַר u-furkan k'hayom hazeh. V'achar
כֵּן בָּאוּ בָנֶיךָ לִדְבִיר בֵּיתֶךָ, kein ba-u vanecha lidvir beitecha
וּפִנּוּ אֶת הֵיכָלֶךָ, וְטִהֲרוּ u-finu et heichalecha v'tiharu
אֶת מִקְדָּשֶׁךָ, וְהִדְלִיקוּ נֵרוֹת et mikdashecha, v'hidliku neirot
בְּחַצְרוֹת קָדְשֶׁךָ וְקָבְעוּ b'chatzrot kodshecha, v'kav'u
שְׁמוֹנַת יְמֵי חֲנֻכָּה אֵלּוּ sh'monat y'mei Chanuka eilu
לְהוֹדוֹת וּלְהַלֵּל לְשִׁמְךָ הַגָּדוֹל: l'hodot ul-haleil l'shimcha hagadol.

In the days of Mattathias ben Johanan, the Hasmonean high priest, and his sons, the wicked Hellenist forces arose to force Israel to forget the Torah and transgress its laws, but God, in God's great mercy, championed Israel's cause and defended them, dealing retribution and delivering the mighty into the hands of the weak, the many into the hands of the few, the impure into the hands of the pure, the wicked into the hands of the righteous, and the tyrants into the hands of the followers of the Torah. By God's great deliverance of Israel God made God's Name great and holy in the world to this very day, for afterward God's people came to the Temple, cleansed and purified the sanctuary, and kindled lights in the holy courts, instituting these eight days of dedication for thanks and praise to God's great name.

On Purim:

בִּימֵי מָרְדְּכַי וְאֶסְתֵּר בְּשׁוּשַׁן
הַבִּירָה, כְּשֶׁעָמַד עֲלֵיהֶם הָמָן
הָרָשָׁע, בִּקֵּשׁ לְהַשְׁמִיד לַהֲרֹג
וּלְאַבֵּד אֶת־כָּל־הַיְּהוּדִים מִנַּעַר
וְעַד־זָקֵן, טַף וְנָשִׁים בְּיוֹם
אֶחָד, בִּשְׁלֹשָׁה עָשָׂר לְחֹדֶשׁ
שְׁנֵים עָשָׂר, הוּא חֹדֶשׁ אֲדָר
וּשְׁלָלָם לָבוֹז. וְאַתָּה
בְּרַחֲמֶיךָ הָרַבִּים הֵפַרְתָּ אֶת
עֲצָתוֹ, וְקִלְקַלְתָּ אֶת מַחֲשַׁבְתּוֹ,
וַהֲשֵׁבוֹתָ גְּמוּלוֹ בְרֹאשׁוֹ, וְתָלוּ
אוֹתוֹ וְאֶת־בָּנָיו עַל הָעֵץ.

Bimei Mordechai v' Ester b'Shushan habira, k'she-amad aleihem Haman ha-rasha, bikeish l'hashmid laharog ul-abeid et kol ha-y'hudim mina-ar v'ad zakein, taf v'nashim b'yom echad, bish-losha asar l'chodesh sh'neim asar hu chodesh Adar ush-lalam lavoz. V'ata b'rachamecha harabim heifarta et atzato v'kilkalta et machashavto, vahasheivota g'mulo b'rosho, v'talu oto v'et banav al ha-eitz.

In Shushan, the Persian capital, in the days of Mordecai and Esther, the wicked Haman arose to slay, despoil and annihilate all the Jews, young and old alike, on the thirteenth of Adar, but God's great mercy frustrated his plan and foiled his plot, causing it to backfire on him so that Haman and his sons were hanged on their own gallows.

On Yom Haatzmaut:

בִּימֵי שִׁיבַת בָּנִים לִגְבוּלָם,
בְּעֵת תְּקוּמַת עַם בְּאַרְצוֹ
כִּימֵי קֶדֶם, נִסְגְּרוּ שַׁעֲרֵי אֶרֶץ
אָבוֹת בִּפְנֵי אַחֵינוּ פְּלִיטֵי חֶרֶב,
וְאוֹיְבִים בָּאָרֶץ וְשִׁבְעָה עֲמָמִים
בַּעֲלֵי בְרִיתָם קָמוּ לְהַכְרִית
עַמְּךָ יִשְׂרָאֵל, וְאַתָּה בְּרַחֲמֶיךָ
הָרַבִּים עָמַדְתָּ לָהֶם בְּעֵת
צָרָתָם, רַבְתָּ אֶת־רִיבָם, דַּנְתָּ

Bimei shivat banim ligvulam, b'eit t'kumat am b'artzo kimei kedem, nisg'ru sha'arei eretz avot bifnei acheinu p'litei cherev v'oyvim ba'aretz v'shiv'a amamim ba'alei v'ritam kamu l'hachrit am'cha Yisra'el, v'ata b'rachamecha harabim amadta lahem b'eit tzaratam, ravta et rivam, danta

אֶת־דִּינָם, חִזַּקְתָּ אֶת־לִבָּם
לַעֲמוֹד בַּשַּׁעַר, וְלִפְתּוֹחַ
שְׁעָרִים לַנִּרְדָּפִים וּלְגָרֵשׁ
אֶת־צִבְאוֹת הָאוֹיֵב מִן הָאָרֶץ.
מָסַרְתָּ רַבִּים בְּיַד מְעַטִּים,
וּרְשָׁעִים בְּיַד צַדִּיקִים, וּלְךָ
עָשִׂיתָ שֵׁם גָּדוֹל וְקָדוֹשׁ
בְּעוֹלָמֶךָ, וּלְעַמְּךָ יִשְׂרָאֵל
עָשִׂיתָ תְּשׁוּעָה גְדוֹלָה וּפֻרְקָן
כְּהַיּוֹם הַזֶּה.

et dinam, chizakta et libam
la'amod basha'ar, v'lifto'ach
sh'arim lanirdafim ul'gareish
et tzvi'ot ha'oyeiv min ha'aretz.
Masarta rabim b'yad m'atim,
ursha'im b'yad tzadikim, ul'cha
asita sheim gadol v'kadosh
b'olamecha, ul'am'cha Yisrael
asita t'shu'a g'dola ufarkan
k'hayom hazeh.

In the days when Your children were returning to their borders, at the time of a people revived in its land as in days of old, the gates to the land of our ancestors were closed before those who were fleeing the sword. When enemies from within the land together with seven neighboring nations sought to annihilate Your people, You, in Your great mercy, stood by them in time of trouble. You defended them and vindicated them. You gave them the courage to meet their foes, to open the gates to those seeking refuge, and to free the land of its armed invaders. You delivered the many into the hands of the few, the guilty into the hands of the innocent. You have wrought great victories and miraculous deliverance for Your people Israel to this day, revealing Your glory and Your holiness to all the world.

וְעַל הַכֹּל, יְיָ אֱלֹהֵינוּ אֲנַחְנוּ
מוֹדִים לָךְ וּמְבָרְכִים אוֹתָךְ,
יִתְבָּרַךְ שִׁמְךָ בְּפִי כָל־חַי
תָּמִיד לְעוֹלָם וָעֶד, כַּכָּתוּב:
"וְאָכַלְתָּ וְשָׂבַעְתָּ וּבֵרַכְתָּ
אֶת־יְיָ אֱלֹהֶיךָ עַל־הָאָרֶץ הַטֹּבָה
אֲשֶׁר נָתַן־לָךְ." בָּרוּךְ אַתָּה
יְיָ, עַל הָאָרֶץ וְעַל הַמָּזוֹן.

V'al hakol, Adonai Eloheinu anachnu
modem lach um-varchim otach
yitbarach shimcha b'fi chol chai
tamid l'olam va-ed, kakatuv:
"V'achalta v'savata u-veirachta
et Adonai Elohecha al ha-aretz hatova
asher natan lach." Baruch atah
Adonai, al ha-aretz v'al hamazon.

For all these blessings we thank the Lord our God and praise God. May God's name be praised by every living being forever, as it is written in God's Torah: "When you have eaten your fill, give thanks to the Lord your God for the good land which God has given you." Blessed is the Lord for the land and its produce.

רַחֵם יי אֱלֹהֵינוּ עַל יִשְׂרָאֵל
עַמֶּךָ, וְעַל יְרוּשָׁלַיִם עִירֶךָ, וְעַל
צִיּוֹן מִשְׁכַּן כְּבוֹדֶךָ וְעַל מַלְכוּת
בֵּית דָּוִד מְשִׁיחֶךָ וְעַל הַבַּיִת
הַגָּדוֹל וְהַקָּדוֹשׁ שֶׁנִּקְרָא
שִׁמְךָ עָלָיו. אֱלֹהֵינוּ אָבִינוּ, רְעֵנוּ
זוּנֵנוּ, פַּרְנְסֵנוּ וְכַלְכְּלֵנוּ,
וְהַרְוִיחֵנוּ, וְהַרְוַח־לָנוּ יי
אֱלֹהֵינוּ מְהֵרָה מִכָּל־צָרוֹתֵינוּ.
וְנָא אַל תַּצְרִיכֵנוּ, יי אֱלֹהֵינוּ,
לֹא לִידֵי מַתְּנַת בָּשָׂר וָדָם וְלֹא
לִידֵי הַלְוָאָתָם, כִּי אִם לְיָדְךָ
הַמְּלֵאָה הַפְּתוּחָה הַגְּדוּשָׁה
וְהָרְחָבָה, שֶׁלֹּא נֵבוֹשׁ וְלֹא
נִכָּלֵם לְעוֹלָם וָעֶד.

Racheim, Adonai Eloheinu, al Yisrael amecha, v'al Y'rushalayim irecha, v'al tzion mishkan, k'vodecha v'al malchut Beit David m'shichecha, v'al habayit hagadol v'hakadosh shenikra shimcha alav. Eloheinu, Avinu, r'einu, zuneinu, parn'seinu, v'chalk'leinu, v'harvicheinu, v'harvach lanu Adonai Eloheinu m'heira mikol tzaroteinu. V'na al tatz-richeinu, Adonai Eloheinu, lo lidei matnat basar vadam v'lo lidei hal-va-a-tam, ki im l'yad'cha ham'lei-a, hap'tucha, hag'dusha, v'har'chava, shelo neivosh v'lo nikaleim l'olam va-ed.

May the Lord our God have mercy on Israel God's people, Jerusalem God's city, Zion the abode of God's glory, the royal house of David God's anointed, and the great and holy Temple that bears God's name. May our God and Father tend and nourish us, sustain and maintain us, and speedily grant us relief from all our troubles. May the Lord our God make us dependent not on the alms or loans of human, but rather on God's full, open and generous hand, so that we may never be humiliated or put to shame.

בשבת

רְצֵה וְהַחֲלִיצֵנוּ יי
אֱלֹהֵינוּ בְּמִצְוֹתֶיךָ, וּבְמִצְוַת
יוֹם הַשְּׁבִיעִי הַשַּׁבָּת הַגָּדוֹל
וְהַקָּדוֹשׁ הַזֶּה. כִּי יוֹם זֶה גָּדוֹל
וְקָדוֹשׁ הוּא לְפָנֶיךָ, לִשְׁבָּת־בּוֹ
וְלָנוּחַ בּוֹ בְּאַהֲבָה כְּמִצְוַת
רְצוֹנֶךָ, וּבִרְצוֹנְךָ הָנִיחַ
לָנוּ, יי אֱלֹהֵינוּ, שֶׁלֹּא תְהֵא
צָרָה וְיָגוֹן וַאֲנָחָה בְּיוֹם
מְנוּחָתֵנוּ. וְהַרְאֵנוּ, יי
אֱלֹהֵינוּ, בְּנֶחָמַת צִיּוֹן
עִירֶךָ, וּבְבִנְיַן יְרוּשָׁלַיִם עִיר
קָדְשֶׁךָ כִּי אַתָּה הוּא בַּעַל
הַיְשׁוּעוֹת וּבַעַל הַנֶּחָמוֹת.

R'tzei v'hachalitzeinu Adonai
Eloheinu b'mizvotecha uv-mitzvat
yom hash'vi-i haShabbat hagadol
v'hakadosh hazeh. Ki yom zeh gadol
v'kadosh hu l'fanecha, lishbot bo
v'lanuach bo b'ahavah k'mitzvat
r'tzonecha. U'virtzon'cha hani'ach
lanu Adonai Eloheinu, shelo t'hei
tzara v'yagon va-anacha b'yom
m'nuchateinu. V'har-einu, Adonai
Eloheinu b'nechamat Tzion
irecha, u'v'vinyan Y'rushalayim ir
kodshecha ki atah hu ba-al
ha-y'shuot u-va-al hanechamot.

May it be God's will to strengthen us in His commandments, especially regarding the seventh day, this great and holy Shabbat, for today is great and holy before God—a day on which to rest and repose in love, according to God's command. May it be God's will to grant us relief from all care, sorrow and grief on our day of rest, and may God enable us to see Zion comforted and Jerusalem, the holy city, rebuilt, for it is God who grants salvation and comfort.

בראש חדש וביום טוב

אֱלֹהֵינוּ וֵאלֹהֵי אֲבוֹתֵינוּ, יַעֲלֶה
וְיָבֹא וְיַגִּיעַ, וְיֵרָאֶה
וְיֵרָצֶה וְיִשָּׁמַע, וְיִפָּקֵד
וְיִזָּכֵר זִכְרוֹנֵנוּ וּפִקְדוֹנֵנוּ,
וְזִכְרוֹן אֲבוֹתֵינוּ, וְזִכְרוֹן
מָשִׁיחַ בֶּן דָּוִד עַבְדֶּךָ,

Eloheinu v'eilohei avoteinu, ya-aleh,
v'yavo, v'yagia, v'yeira-eh,
v'yeiratzeh, v'yishama, v'yipakeid,
v'yizacheir zichroneinu u-fikdoneinu,
v'zichron avoteinu, v'zichron
Mashiach ben David avdecha,

וְזִכְרוֹן יְרוּשָׁלַיִם עִיר קָדְשֶׁךָ,　v'zichron Y'rushalayim ir kodshecha,
וְזִכְרוֹן כָּל עַמְּךָ בֵּית יִשְׂרָאֵל　v'zichron kol am'cha beit Yisrael
לְפָנֶיךָ, לִפְלֵיטָה לְטוֹבָה, וּלְחֵן　l'fanecha, lif-leita ul-tova, ul-chein
וּלְחֶסֶד וּלְרַחֲמִים לְחַיִּים　ul-chesed ul-rachamim l-chayim
וּלְשָׁלוֹם –　ul-shalom –

May remembrance and mindfulness of us and of our ancestors, of the Messiah, son of David, God's servant, of Jerusalem, God's holy city, and of all God's people, the house of Israel, come before our God and be remembered and accepted with mercy and kindness, life and peace, on this day of ...

בְּיוֹם:　*Add for appropriate day:*

ר"ח　*On Rosh Chodesh say:*

בְּיוֹם רֹאשׁ הַחֹדֶשׁ הַזֶּה.　B'yom Rosh Hachodesh hazeh.
the New Month.

פסח　*On Pesach say:*

בְּיוֹם חַג הַמַּצּוֹת הַזֶּה.　B'yom Chag Hamatzot hazeh.
the Festival of Unleavened Bread.

שבועות　*On Shavu'ot say:*

בְּיוֹם חַג הַשָּׁבֻעוֹת הַזֶּה.　B'yom Chag Hashavuot hazeh.
the Festival of Weeks.

ר"ה　*On Rosh Hashanah say:*

בְּיוֹם הַזִּכְרוֹן הַזֶּה.　B'yom Hazikaron hazeh.
Day of Remembrance.

סוכות　*On Sukkot say:*

בְּיוֹם חַג הַסֻּכּוֹת הַזֶּה.　B'yom Chag Hasukkot hazeh.
the Festival of Booths.

On Sh'mini Atzeret and
Simchat Torah say:

בְּיוֹם הַשְּׁמִינִי חַג
הָעֲצֶרֶת הַזֶּה.

B'yom Hash'mini Chag
Ha-atzeret hazeh.

the Closing Festival.

זָכְרֵנוּ, יי אֱלֹהֵינוּ, בּוֹ
לְטוֹבָה, וּפָקְדֵנוּ בוֹ לִבְרָכָה,
וְהוֹשִׁיעֵנוּ בוֹ לְחַיִּים.
וּבִדְבַר יְשׁוּעָה וְרַחֲמִים
חוּס וְחָנֵּנוּ, וְרַחֵם עָלֵינוּ
וְהוֹשִׁיעֵנוּ, כִּי אֵלֶיךָ עֵינֵינוּ, כִּי
אֵל מֶלֶךְ חַנּוּן וְרַחוּם אָתָּה.

Zochreinu, Adonai Eloheinu, bo
l'tova, u-fokdeinu vo livracha,
v'hoshi-einu vo l'chayim.
u-vidvar y'shua v'rachamim
chus v'choneinu v'racheim aleinu
v'hoshi-einu ki eilecha eineinu, ki
Eil melech chanun v'rachum atah.

May God remember us for good, grant us blessing and preserve us in life.
May God show us compassion and grace with the promise of salvation and
mercy. May God be merciful toward us and save us, for our eyes are turned
to a gracious and merciful God.

וּבְנֵה יְרוּשָׁלַיִם עִיר הַקֹּדֶשׁ
בִּמְהֵרָה בְיָמֵינוּ. בָּרוּךְ
אַתָּה יי, בּוֹנֵה בְרַחֲמָיו
יְרוּשָׁלַיִם. אָמֵן.

Uv-nei Y'rushalayim ir Hakodesh
bimheira v'yameinu. Baruch
atah Adonai, boneh v'rachamav
Y'rushalayim. Amein.

May God rebuild Jerusalem, the holy city, speedily in our lifetime. Blessed is
the Lord, who in God's mercy restores Jerusalem. Amen.

בָּרוּךְ אַתָּה יי אֱלֹהֵינוּ מֶלֶךְ
הָעוֹלָם, הָאֵל, אָבִינוּ מַלְכֵּנוּ,
אַדִּירֵנוּ בּוֹרְאֵנוּ, גֹּאֲלֵנוּ,
יוֹצְרֵנוּ, קְדוֹשֵׁנוּ קְדוֹשׁ יַעֲקֹב,
רוֹעֵנוּ רוֹעֵה יִשְׂרָאֵל, הַמֶּלֶךְ
הַטּוֹב וְהַמֵּטִיב לַכֹּל, שֶׁבְּכָל-יוֹם

Baruch atah Adonai Eloheinu melech
ha-olam ha-Eil, avinu malkeinu,
adireinu, bor'einu, go-aleinu,
yotz-reinu, k'dosheinu k'dosh Ya'akov,
ro-einu ro-ei Yisrael, hamelech hatov
v'hameitiv lakol, she-b'chol yom

וְיוֹם הוּא הֵטִיב, הוּא מֵטִיב, vayom hu heitiv, hu meitiv,
הוּא יֵיטִיב לָנוּ. הוּא גְמָלָנוּ הוּא hu yeitiv lanu. Hu g'malanu Hu
גוֹמְלֵנוּ, הוּא יִגְמְלֵנוּ לָעַד, gomleinu, Hu yig-m'leinu, la-ad,
לְחֵן, וּלְחֶסֶד, וּלְרַחֲמִים, l'chein, ul-chesed, ul-rachamin,
וּלְרֶוַח, הַצָּלָה וְהַצְלָחָה, בְּרָכָה ul-revach, hatzala v-hatzlacha, b'racha
וִישׁוּעָה, נֶחָמָה, פַּרְנָסָה vi-shua, nechama, parnasa,
וְכַלְכָּלָה, וְרַחֲמִים וְחַיִּים v'chalkala v'rachamim, v'chayim,
וְשָׁלוֹם וְכָל־טוֹב, וּמִכָּל־טוּב v'shalom, v'chol tov, u-mikol tuv
לְעוֹלָם אַל יְחַסְּרֵנוּ. l'olam al y'chasreinu.

Blessed is the Lord our God, King of the universe, who is our God, our
Sovereign, our King, our Mighty One, our Creator, our Redeemer, our Maker,
the Holy one of Jacob, the Shepherd of Israel, the good Sovereign who does
good to all. May God who continually shows us kindness continue God's
goodness to us. As God has ever bestowed God's favors upon us, may God
continue to bless us with grace, lovingkindness, compassion and deliverance,
prosperity, redemption, and consolation, sustenance, and mercy, a life of peace
and all goodness. May God never withhold God's goodness from us.

הָרַחֲמָן, הוּא יִמְלֹךְ עָלֵינוּ Harachaman hu yimloch aleinu
לְעוֹלָם וָעֶד. l'olam va-ed.

הָרַחֲמָן, הוּא יִתְבָּרַךְ Harachaman hu yitbarach
בַּשָּׁמַיִם וּבָאָרֶץ. bashamayim u-va-aretz.

הָרַחֲמָן, הוּא יִשְׁתַּבַּח לְדוֹר Harachaman hu yishtabach l'dor
דּוֹרִים, וְיִתְפָּאַר בָּנוּ לָעַד dorim v'yitpa-ar banu la-ad
לָנֶצַח נְצָחִים, וְיִתְהַדַּר l'neitzach n'tzachim, v'yit-hadar
בָּנוּ לָעַד וּלְעוֹלְמֵי עוֹלָמִים. banu la-ad ul-ol'mei olamim.

הָרַחֲמָן, הוּא יְפַרְנְסֵנוּ Harachaman, hu y'far-n'seinu
בְּכָבוֹד. b'chavod.

הָרַחֲמָן, הוּא יִשְׁבּוֹר עֻלֵּנוּ
מֵעַל צַוָּארֵנוּ וְהוּא יוֹלִיכֵנוּ
קוֹמְמִיּוּת לְאַרְצֵנוּ.

Harachaman, hu yishbor uleinu
mei-al tzavareinu v'hu yolicheinu
kom'miyut l'artzeinu.

הָרַחֲמָן, הוּא יִשְׁלַח בְּרָכָה
מְרֻבָּה בַּבַּיִת הַזֶּה, וְעַל
שֻׁלְחָן זֶה שֶׁאָכַלְנוּ עָלָיו.

Harachaman, hu yishlach bracha
m'ruba ba bayit hazeh ve'al shulchan
zeh, she'achalnu alav.

הָרַחֲמָן, הוּא יִשְׁלַח לָנוּ אֶת
אֵלִיָּהוּ הַנָּבִיא, זָכוּר לַטּוֹב,
וִיבַשֶּׂר לָנוּ בְּשׂוֹרוֹת טוֹבוֹת
יְשׁוּעוֹת וְנֶחָמוֹת.

Harachaman, hu yishlach lanu et
Eliyahu hanavi, zachur la tov,
vivaser lanu b'sorot tovot
y'shu-ot v'nechamot.

May God reign over us forever and ever.

May God be extolled in heaven and on earth.

May God be praised in all generations, may God be glorified through us to all eternity; may God be honored among us forever.

May God grant us an honorable livelihood.

May God break the yoke of our oppression and lead us in dignity to our ancient homeland.

May God send abundant blessing upon this dwelling and the table at which we have eaten.

May God send Elijah the Prophet to us, and may he bear good tidings of salvation and comfort.

When eating at one's own table say:

הָרַחֲמָן, הוּא יְבָרֵךְ אוֹתִי
וְאֶת־כָּל אֲשֶׁר לִי־
(וְאֶת־אִשְׁתִּי\בַּעֲלִי וְאֶת־זַרְעִי)
אוֹתָנוּ וְאֶת־כָּל אֲשֶׁר לָנוּ־

Harachaman hu y'vareich oti
v'et kol asher li
(v'et ishti/v'et ba'ali ve'et zar-i)
otanu v'et kol asher lanu-

May God bless me (my wife/my husband, my children) and all my family.

60

When eating at another's table say

(when eating at one's parents' table include the words in parentheses):

הָרַחֲמָן, הוּא יְבָרֵךְ אֶת־
(אָבִי מוֹרִי) בַּעַל הַבַּיִת הַזֶּה,
וְאֶת־(אִמִּי מוֹרָתִי) בַּעֲלַת הַבַּיִת
הַזֶּה, אוֹתָם וְאֶת־בֵּיתָם
וְאֶת־זַרְעָם וְאֶת־כָּל־אֲשֶׁר לָהֶם־

Harachaman, hu y'vareich et
(avi mori) ba-al habayit hazeh,
V'et (imi morati) ba-alat habayit
hazeh, otam v'et beitam
v'et zar-am v'et kol asher lahem-

May God bless (my father, my teacher) the head of this household, and (my mother, my teacher) the head of this household, their children and all their family.

When eating at a communal meal, say:

הָרַחֲמָן, הוּא יְבָרֵךְ אֶת־כָּל־
הַמְסֻבִּין כָּאן, אוֹתָנוּ וְאֶת־כָּל־
אֲשֶׁר לָנוּ--

Harachaman, hu y'vareich et kol
ham'subin kan, otanu v'et kol
asher lanu—

At all meals, continue here:

כְּמוֹ שֶׁנִּתְבָּרְכוּ אֲבוֹתֵינוּ אַבְרָהָם
יִצְחָק וְיַעֲקֹב (וְאִמּוֹתֵנוּ שָׂרָה,
רִבְקָה, רָחֵל, וְלֵאָה) "בַּכֹּל מִכֹּל
כֹּל," כֵּן יְבָרֵךְ אוֹתָנוּ כֻּלָּנוּ יַחַד
בִּבְרָכָה שְׁלֵמָה, וְנֹאמַר אָמֵן.

k'mo she-nitbarchu avoteinu Avraham
Yitzchak v'Ya-akov (v'imoteinu Sarah,
Rivka, Rachel v'Leah), "bakol mikol kol,"
kein y'vareich otanu kulanu yachad
bivracha sh'leima v'nomar Amein.

May God bless all who are gathered here and all their families, as well as all dear to us. Even as our forefathers, Abraham, Isaac and Jacob (and our foremothers, Sarah, Rebecca, Rachel, and Leah) were blessed in every way; so may God bless all of us together with a perfect blessing, and let us say, Amen.

בַּמָּרוֹם יְלַמְּדוּ, עֲלֵיהֶם וְעָלֵינוּ
זְכוּת, שֶׁתְּהֵא לְמִשְׁמֶרֶת שָׁלוֹם.
וְנִשָּׂא בְרָכָה מֵאֵת יי,
וּצְדָקָה מֵאֱלֹהֵי יִשְׁעֵנוּ, וְנִמְצָא
חֵן וְשֵׂכֶל טוֹב בְּעֵינֵי אֱלֹהִים
וְאָדָם.

Bamarom y'lamdu aleihem v'aleinu
z'chut she't'hei l'mishmeret shalom.
V'nisa v'racha mei-eit Adonai,
utz-daka mei-Elohei yisheinu, v'nimtza
chein v'seichel tov B'einei Elohim
v'adam.

May our merit and the merit of our ancestors secure enduring peace for all of us. May we receive a blessing from the Lord, and justice from the God of our salvation. May we find grace and favor in the sight of God and man.

בשבת:

On Shabbat add:

הָרַחֲמָן, הוּא יַנְחִילֵנוּ יוֹם
שֶׁכֻּלוֹ שַׁבָּת וּמְנוּחָה, לְחַיֵּי
הָעוֹלָמִים.

Harachaman, hu yan-chileinu
yom she-kulo Shabbat um-nucha,
l'chayei ha-olamim.

May the Merciful One grant us a world that shall
be entirely Shabbat and eternal rest.

בראש חדש:

On Rosh Chodesh add:

הָרַחֲמָן, הוּא יְחַדֵּשׁ עָלֵינוּ
אֶת־הַחֹדֶשׁ הַזֶּה לְטוֹבָה
וְלִבְרָכָה.

Harachaman, hu y'chadeish
aleinu et hachodesh hazeh l'tovah
v'livracha.

May the Merciful One grant us this new month for good and blessing.

ביום טוב:

On Festivals add:

הָרַחֲמָן, הוּא יַנְחִילֵנוּ יוֹם
שֶׁכֻּלוֹ טוֹב.

Harachaman, hu yan-chileinu yom
she-kulo tov.

May the Merciful One grant us the day that will be entirely good.

בסוכות:

On Sukkot add:

הָרַחֲמָן, הוּא יָקִים לָנוּ אֶת
סֻכַּת דָּוִד הַנֹּפָלֶת.

Harachaman, hu yakim lanu et
sukkat David hanofelet.

May the Merciful One erect the fallen Sukkah of David for us.

בראש השנה:

On Rosh Hashanah add:

הָרַחֲמָן, הוּא יְחַדֵּשׁ עָלֵינוּ
אֶת־הַשָּׁנָה הַזֹּאת לְטוֹבָה
וְלִבְרָכָה.

Harachaman, hu y'chadeish aleinu
et Hashanah hazot l'tovah
v'livracha.

May the Merciful One grant us this year for good and blessing.

הָרַחֲמָן, הוּא יְבָרֵךְ אֶת־מְדִינַת
יִשְׂרָאֵל, רֵאשִׁית צְמִיחַת גְּאֻלָּתֵנוּ.

Harachaman, hu y'vareich et M'dinat
Yisrael, reishit tz'michat g'u-lateinu.

May the Merciful One bless the State of Israel, the dawn of our redemption.

To be recited in the country in which one resides:

הָרַחֲמָן, הוּא יְבָרֵךְ אֶת־הָאָרֶץ
הַזֹּאת וְיָגֵן עָלֶיהָ.

Harachaman, hu y'vareich et ha-aretz
hazot v'yagein aleha.

May the Merciful One bless this land and protect it.

הָרַחֲמָן, הוּא יְבָרֵךְ אֶת־אַחֵינוּ
בְּנֵי יִשְׂרָאֵל הַנְּתוּנִים בְּצָרָה,
וְיוֹצִיאֵם מֵאֲפֵלָה לְאוֹרָה.

Harachaman, hu y'vareich et acheinu
b'nei Yisrael han'tunim betzarah,
v'yotzi-eim mei-afeila l'orah.

May the Merciful One bless all of our people who suffer and bring them out
of darkness into light.

הָרַחֲמָן, הוּא יְזַכֵּנוּ לִימוֹת
הַמָּשִׁיחַ, וּלְחַיֵּי הָעוֹלָם הַבָּא.

Harachaman, hu y'zakeinu limot
haMashiach, ul-chayei ha-olam haba.

May the Merciful One enable us to live in the days of the Messiah and in the
World to Come.

(בחול) מַגְדִּיל
(בשבת, ראש חדש ויום טוב)
מִגְדּוֹל
יְשׁוּעוֹת מַלְכּוֹ, וְעוֹשֶׂה חֶסֶד
לִמְשִׁיחוֹ, לְדָוִד וּלְזַרְעוֹ עַד
עוֹלָם. עוֹשֶׂה שָׁלוֹם בִּמְרוֹמָיו,
הוּא יַעֲשֶׂה שָׁלוֹם עָלֵינוּ וְעַל
כָּל־יִשְׂרָאֵל, וְאִמְרוּ אָמֵן.

Weekdays: Magdil
On Shabbat, Rosh Chodesh & Festivals:
Migdol
y'shu-ot malko, v'oseh chesed
lim-shicho, l'David ul-zar-o ad
olam. Oseh shalom bimromav,
hu ya-aseh shalom aleinu v'al
kol Yisrael, v'imru amein.

God grants deliverance (on Shabbat, Rosh Chodesh and Festivals: God is a
tower of deliverance) to God's chosen, and shows a kindness to God's anointed
one, to David, and his descendents forever. May God who creates peace above,
create peace for us and all Israel, and let us say, Amen.

יְראוּ אֶת־יי קְדוֹשָׁיו, כִּי אֵין
מַחְסוֹר לִירֵאָיו. כְּפִירִים רָשׁוּ
וְרָעֵבוּ וְדֹרְשֵׁי יי לֹא יַחְסְרוּ
כָל־טוֹב. הוֹדוּ לַיי כִּי טוֹב,
כִּי לְעוֹלָם חַסְדּוֹ. פּוֹתֵחַ אֶת־
יָדֶךָ, וּמַשְׂבִּיעַ לְכָל־חַי רָצוֹן.
בָּרוּךְ הַגֶּבֶר אֲשֶׁר יִבְטַח
בַּיי, וְהָיָה יי מִבְטַחוֹ.
נַעַר הָיִיתִי גַם זָקַנְתִּי, וְלֹא
רָאִיתִי צַדִּיק נֶעֱזָב וְזַרְעוֹ מְבַקֶּשׁ
לָחֶם. יי עֹז לְעַמּוֹ יִתֵּן, יי
יְבָרֵךְ אֶת־עַמּוֹ בַשָּׁלוֹם.

Y'ru et Adonai k'doshav, ki ein
machzor lirei-av. K'firim rashu
v'ra-eivu v'dorshei Adonai lo yach-s'ru
chol tov. Hodu Ladonai ki tov,
ki l'olam chasdo. Potei-ach et
yadecha, u-masbia l'chol chai ratzon.
Baruch hagever asher yivtach
Badonai, v'haya Adonai mivtacho.
Na-ar hayiti gam zakanti, v'lo
ra'iti tzadik ne-ezav v'zar-o m'vakesh
lachem. Adonai oz l'amo yitein, Adonai
y'vareich et amo vashalom.

Revere the Lord, you who are God's holy ones.
For those who revere God suffer no want.
Those who deny God may famish and starve,
But they who seek the Lord shall not lack anything that is good.
God's mercy endures forever.
God opens God's hand and satisfies every living thing with favor.

Blessed is the one who trusts in the Lord,
For the Lord will be his protection.
I have been young, and I have grown older,
But I have not seen the righteous man forsaken,
Nor his children begging for bread.
The Lord will give strength to God's people.
The Lord will bless God's people with peace.

זִמּוּן בְּסְעוּדַת נִשּׂוּאִין BIRKAT HAMAZON
GRACE AFTER MEALS AT WEDDINGS

For this special Grace After Meals two cups of wine and an empty cup will be used. At a wedding meal, the Grace After Meals begins here, with the first cup of wine.

Leader:

חֲבֵרַי נְבָרֵךְ   Chaverei n'vareich

Friends, let us thank God.

Group, then leader repeats:

יְהִי שֵׁם יי מְבֹרָךְ   Y'hi sheim Adonai m'vorach

מֵעַתָּה וְעַד עוֹלָם.   mei-ata v'ad olam.

Blessed is the name of the Lord from now and forever.

Leader:

דְּוַי הָסֵר וְגַם חָרוֹן, וְאָז אִלֵּם   D'vai haseir v'gam charon v'az ileim

בְּשִׁיר יָרוֹן, נְחֵנוּ בְּמַעְגְּלֵי   b'shir yaron, n'cheinu b'ma-g'lei

צֶדֶק, שְׁעֵה בִּרְכַּת בְּנֵי אַהֲרֹן.   tzedek, sh'ei birkat b'nei Aharon.

בִּרְשׁוּת חֲבֵרַי, נְבָרֵךְ אֱלֹהֵינוּ   Birshut chaverei n'vareich Eloheinu

שֶׁהַשִּׂמְחָה בִּמְעוֹנוֹ וְשֶׁאָכַלְנוּ   she-hasimcha bim-ono v'she-achalnu

מִשֶּׁלוֹ.   mishelo.

Sweep away sadness and anger, then even the dumb will cry out in song. Guide us in the paths of righteousness. Accept the blessing of the sons of Aaron.

With consent of all present, let us bless our God in whose presence the celebration is, and whose food we have eaten.

Group, then leader repeats:

בָּרוּךְ אֱלֹהֵינוּ שֶׁהַשִּׂמְחָה   Baruch Eloheinu she-hasimcha

בִּמְעוֹנוֹ, וְשֶׁאָכַלְנוּ מִשֶּׁלוֹ   bim'ono v'she-achalnu mishelo

וּבְטוּבוֹ חָיִינוּ.   uv-tuvo chayinu.

65

Blessed is our God in whose presence the celebration is and whose food we have eaten, and through whose goodness we live.

All:

בָּרוּךְ הוּא וּבָרוּךְ שְׁמוֹ׃ Baruch hu uvaruch sh'mo.

May God be blessed and may God's name be blessed.

Grace After Meals continues on page 50.

שבע ברכות SHEVA B'RACHOT

Immediately following the Grace After Meals at the wedding meal, the first six blessings are recited over the second cup of wine by friends and relatives. This second cup of wine is passed from one to another as the blessings are recited.

בָּרוּךְ אַתָּה יי אֱלֹהֵינוּ מֶלֶךְ 1 Baruch atah Adonai Eloheinu melech
הָעוֹלָם, שֶׁהַכֹּל בָּרָא לִכְבוֹדוֹ. ha-olam, she-hakol bara lichvodo.

Praised are You, Lord our God, Sovereign of the universe, who created all things for Your glory.

בָּרוּךְ אַתָּה יי אֱלֹהֵינוּ מֶלֶךְ 2 Baruch atah Adonai Eloheinu melech
הָעוֹלָם, יוֹצֵר הָאָדָם. ha-olam, yotzeir ha-adam.

Praised are You, Lord our God, Sovereign of the universe, Creator of human.

בָּרוּךְ אַתָּה יי אֱלֹהֵינוּ מֶלֶךְ Baruch atah Adonai Eloheinu melech
הָעוֹלָם, אֲשֶׁר יָצַר אֶת־הָאָדָם ha-olam, asher yatzar et ha-adam
בְּצַלְמוֹ, בְּצֶלֶם דְּמוּת תַּבְנִיתוֹ, 3 b'tzalmo, b'tzelem d'mut tavnito,
וְהִתְקִין לוֹ מִמֶּנּוּ בִּנְיַן עֲדֵי עַד. v'hitkin lo mimenu binyan adei ad.
בָּרוּךְ אַתָּה יי, יוֹצֵר הָאָדָם. Baruch atah Adonai, yotzeir ha-adam.

Praised are You, Lord our God, Sovereign of the universe, who created man and woman in Your image, fashioning woman from man as his mate, that together they might perpetuate life. Praised are You, Lord, Creator of human.

66

שׂוֹשׂ תָּשִׂישׂ וְתָגֵל הָעֲקָרָה,
בְּקִבּוּץ בָּנֶיהָ לְתוֹכָהּ בְּשִׂמְחָה.
בָּרוּךְ אַתָּה יי, מְשַׂמֵּחַ
צִיּוֹן בְּבָנֶיהָ.

Sos tasis v'tageil ha-akara
b'kibutz baneha l'tocha b'simcha.
Baruch atah Adonai, m'samei-ach
Tzion b'vaneiha.

4

May Zion rejoice as her children are restored to her in joy. Praised are You Lord, who causes Zion to rejoice at her children's return.

שַׂמֵּחַ תְּשַׂמַּח רֵעִים
הָאֲהוּבִים, כְּשַׂמֵּחֲךָ יְצִירְךָ
בְּגַן עֵדֶן מִקֶּדֶם. בָּרוּךְ
אַתָּה יי, מְשַׂמֵּחַ
חָתָן וְכַלָּה.

Samei-ach t'samach rei-im
ha-ahuvim k'samei-cha-cha y'tzircha
b'gan eiden mikedem. Baruch
atah Adonai, m'samei-ach
chatan v'chalah.

5

Grant perfect joy to these loving companions, as You did to the first man and woman in the Garden of Eden. Praised are You, Lord, who grants the joy of bride and groom.

בָּרוּךְ אַתָּה יי
אֱלֹהֵינוּ מֶלֶךְ הָעוֹלָם,
אֲשֶׁר בָּרָא שָׂשׂוֹן וְשִׂמְחָה,
חָתָן וְכַלָּה,
גִּילָה, רִנָּה, דִּיצָה וְחֶדְוָה,
אַהֲבָה וְאַחֲוָה, וְשָׁלוֹם וְרֵעוּת.
מְהֵרָה, יי אֱלֹהֵינוּ,
יִשָּׁמַע בְּעָרֵי יְהוּדָה
וּבְחֻצוֹת יְרוּשָׁלָיִם
קוֹל שָׂשׂוֹן וְקוֹל שִׂמְחָה,
קוֹל חָתָן וְקוֹל כַּלָּה,
קוֹל מִצְהֲלוֹת חֲתָנִים מֵחֻפָּתָם
וּנְעָרִים מִמִּשְׁתֵּה נְגִינָתָם.
בָּרוּךְ אַתָּה יי, מְשַׂמֵּחַ
חָתָן עִם הַכַּלָּה.

Baruch atah Adonai
Eloheinu melech ha-olam,
asher bara sason v'simcha
chatan v'chalah,
gilah rinah ditzah v'chedvah,
ahavah v'achavah v'shalom v'rei-ut.
M'heira Adonai Eloheinu
yishama b'arei Y'hudah
u-v'chutzot Y'rushalayim
kol sason v'kol simcha,
kol chatan v'kol kalah,
kol mitz-halot chatanim meichupatam
un-arim mimichtei n'ginatam.
Baruch atah Adonai, m'samei-ach
chatan im hakalah.

6

67

Praised are You, Lord our God, Sovereign of the universe, who created joy and gladness, bride and groom, mirth, song, delight and rejoicing, love and harmony, peace and companionship. Speedily, Lord our God, may there ever be heard in the cities of Judah and in the streets of Jerusalem voices of joy and gladness, voices of bride and groom, the jubilant voices of those joined in marriage under the bridal canopy, the voices of young people feasting and singing. Praised are You, Lord, who causes the groom to rejoice with his bride.

The leader of the Grace After Meals lifts the first cup of wine and recites:

בָּרוּךְ אַתָּה יי אֱלֹהֵינוּ   Baruch atah Adonai, Eloheinu
מֶלֶךְ הָעוֹלָם, בּוֹרֵא פְּרִי הַגָּפֶן.   melech ha-olam, borei p'ri hagafen.

Praised are You, Lord our God, Sovereign of the universe, Creator of the fruit of the vine.

Wine from each of the two cups is mixed together into a third cup. Some wine from the third cup is then poured back into each of the first two cups. One cup of wine is given to the bride to drink, one is given to the bridegroom to drink and one is given to the leader to drink.

ברכת המזון מקוצרת BIRKAT HAMAZON
ABRIDGED VERSION

On Shabbat, Shir Hama'alot is said (see page 47)
When three or more have eaten together (Word in parentheses is recited only when there is a minyan present):

Leader:

חֲבֵרַי נְבָרֵךְ   Chaverei n'vareich

Friends let us give thanks.

Group, then Leader Repeats:

יְהִי שֵׁם יי מְבֹרָךְ   Y'hi sheim Adonai m'vorach
מֵעַתָּה וְעַד עוֹלָם.   mei-atah v'ad olam.

May the Lord be praised, now and forever.

Leader:

בִּרְשׁוּת חֲבֵרַי, נְבָרֵךְ (אֱלֹהֵינוּ)   Birshut Chaverei, n'vareich (Eloheinu)
שֶׁאָכַלְנוּ מִשֶּׁלוֹ.   she-achalnu mishelo.

With your consent, friends, let us praise God
of whose food we have partaken.

Group, then Leader Repeats:

בָּרוּךְ (אֱלֹהֵינוּ) שֶׁאָכַלְנוּ   Baruch (Eloheinu) she-achalnu
מִשֶּׁלוֹ וּבְטוּבוֹ חָיִינוּ.   mishelo uvtuvo chayinu.

Praised be our God of whose food we have partaken
and by whose goodness we live.

All:

בָּרוּךְ הוּא וּבָרוּךְ שְׁמוֹ:   Baruch hu u-varuch sh'mo.

Praised be God and praised be God's name:

69

בָּרוּךְ אַתָּה יי אֱלֹהֵינוּ מֶלֶךְ
הָעוֹלָם, הַזָּן אֶת־הָעוֹלָם כֻּלּוֹ
בְּטוּבוֹ בְּחֵן בְּחֶסֶד וּבְרַחֲמִים.
הוּא נוֹתֵן לֶחֶם לְכָל־בָּשָׂר, כִּי
לְעוֹלָם חַסְדּוֹ. וּבְטוּבוֹ הַגָּדוֹל
תָּמִיד לֹא חָסַר לָנוּ, וְאַל יֶחְסַר־
לָנוּ מָזוֹן לְעוֹלָם וָעֶד. בַּעֲבוּר
שְׁמוֹ הַגָּדוֹל, כִּי הוּא אֵל זָן
וּמְפַרְנֵס לַכֹּל, וּמֵטִיב לַכֹּל,
וּמֵכִין מָזוֹן לְכָל־בְּרִיּוֹתָיו אֲשֶׁר
בָּרָא. בָּרוּךְ אַתָּה יי, הַזָּן
אֶת־הַכֹּל.

Baruch atah Adonai Eloheinu melech
ha-olam, hazan et ha-olam kulo
b'tuvo b'chein b'chesed uv-rachamim,
Hu notein lechem l'chol basar, ki
l'olam chasdo. Uv-tuvo hagadol
tamid lo chaser lanu v'al yechsar
lanu mazon l'olam va-ed. Ba-avur
sh'mo hagadol ki hu el zan
um-farneis lakol u-meitiv lakol
u-meichin mazon l'chol b'riyotav asher
bara. Baruch atah Adonai, hazan
et hakol.

Blessed is the Lord our God, Sovereign of the universe, who sustains the entire
world with goodness, kindness and mercy. God gives food to all creatures, for
God's mercy is everlasting. Through God's abundant goodness we have never yet
been in want; may we never be in want of sustenance for the sake of God's great
name. God sustains all, does good to all, and provides food for all the creatures
whom God has created. Blessed is the Lord, who provides food for all.

נוֹדֶה לְךָ, יי אֱלֹהֵינוּ, עַל
שֶׁהִנְחַלְתָּ לַאֲבוֹתֵינוּ אֶרֶץ
חֶמְדָּה טוֹבָה וּרְחָבָה, בְּרִית
וְתוֹרָה, חַיִּים וּמָזוֹן. יִתְבָּרַךְ
שִׁמְךָ בְּפִי כָל־חַי תָּמִיד לְעוֹלָם
וָעֶד, כַּכָּתוּב: "וְאָכַלְתָּ וְשָׂבָעְתָּ
וּבֵרַכְתָּ אֶת־יי אֱלֹהֶיךָ
עַל־הָאָרֶץ הַטֹּבָה
אֲשֶׁר נָתַן־לָךְ." בָּרוּךְ אַתָּה
יי, עַל הָאָרֶץ וְעַל הַמָּזוֹן.

Nodeh l'cha, Adonai Eloheinu al
she-hinchalta la-avoteinu eretz
chemda tova ur-chava, b'rit
v'Torah, chayim u-mazon. Yitbarach
shimcha b'fi chol chai tamid l'olam
va-ed, kakatuv: "V'achalta v'savata
u-veirachta et Adonai Elohecha"
al ha-aretz hatova
asher natan lach. Baruch atah
Adonai, al ha-aretz v'al hamazon.

We thank You, Lord our God, for the pleasing, ample, desirable land which You gave to our ancestors, for the covenant and Torah, for life and sustenance. May You forever be praised by all who live, as it is written in the Torah: "When you have eaten your fill, you shall praise the Lord your God for the good land which God has given you. "Praised are You, Lord, for the land and for sustenance.

On Shabbat, Rosh Chodesh or Festivals, add the appropriate paragraph from the full Birkat Hamazon (pages 51-54 or 56-58)

וּבְנֵה יְרוּשָׁלַיִם עִיר הַקֹּדֶשׁ
בִּמְהֵרָה בְיָמֵינוּ. בָּרוּךְ אַתָּה
יי, בּוֹנֵה בְרַחֲמָיו
יְרוּשָׁלָיִם. אָמֵן.

Uv-nei Y'rushalayim ir hakodesh
bimheira v'yameinu. Baruch atah
Adonai, boneh v'rachamav
Y'rushalayim. Amein.

Build up Jerusalem, the holy city, in our time. Praised are You, Lord, who in the Lord's mercy rebuilds Jerusalem. Amein.

בָּרוּךְ אַתָּה יי אֱלֹהֵינוּ מֶלֶךְ
הָעוֹלָם, הַמֶּלֶךְ הַטּוֹב וְהַמֵּטִיב
לַכֹּל. הוּא הֵטִיב, הוּא מֵטִיב,
הוּא יֵיטִיב לָנוּ. הוּא גְמָלָנוּ,
הוּא גוֹמְלֵנוּ הוּא יִגְמְלֵנוּ לָעַד,
חֵן וָחֶסֶד וְרַחֲמִים,
וִיזַכֵּנוּ לִימוֹת הַמָּשִׁיחַ.

Baruch atah Adonai, Eloheinu melech
ha-olam, hamelech hatov v'hameitiv
lakol. Hu heitiv, hu meitiv,
hu yeitiv lanu. Hu g'malanu,
hu gom-leinu, hu yigm'leinu la-ad,
chein va'chesed v'rachamim,
vi-zakeinu limot hamashi-ach.

Praised are You, Lord our God, Sovereign of the universe, who is good to all, whose goodness is constant throughout all time. Favor us with kindness and compassion now and in the future as in the past. May we be worthy of the days of the Messiah.

בשבת: *On Shabbat:*

הָרַחֲמָן, הוּא יַנְחִילֵנוּ יוֹם
שֶׁכֻּלוֹ שַׁבָּת וּמְנוּחָה,
לְחַיֵּי הָעוֹלָמִים.

Harachaman, hu yan-chileinu yom
she-kulo Shabbat um-nucha-
l'chayei ha-olamim.

May the Merciful grant us a day of true Shabbat rest,
reflecting the life of eternity.

בראש חדש: *On Rosh Chodesh:*

הָרַחֲמָן, הוּא יְחַדֵּשׁ עָלֵינוּ
אֶת־הַחֹדֶשׁ הַזֶּה לְטוֹבָה
וְלִבְרָכָה.

Harachaman, hu y'chadeish aleinu
et hachodesh hazeh l'tovah
v'livracha.

May the Merciful renew this month for goodness and blessing.

ביום טוב: *On Festivals:*

הָרַחֲמָן, הוּא יַנְחִילֵנוּ
יוֹם שֶׁכֻּלוֹ טוֹב.

Harachaman, hu yan-chileinu
yom shekulo tov.

May the Merciful grant us a day fulfilled with the spirit of the Festival.

בראש השנה: *On Rosh Hashanah:*

הָרַחֲמָן, הוּא יְחַדֵּשׁ עָלֵינוּ
אֶת־הַשָּׁנָה הַזֹּאת לְטוֹבָה
וְלִבְרָכָה.

Harachaman, hu yechadesh aleinu
et hashana hazot l'tova
ve'livracha.

May the Merciful renew for us this year in goodness and blessing.

בסוכות: *On Sukkot:*

הָרַחֲמָן, הוּא יָקִים לָנוּ
אֶת־סֻכַּת דָּוִד הַנֹּפֶלֶת.

Harachaman, hu yakim lanu
et sukkat David hanofelet.

May the Merciful raise the fallen sukkah of David.

72

On *Chanukah*:

הָרַחֲמָן, הוּא יַעֲשֶׂה לָנוּ נִסִּים
Harachaman, hu ya-aseh lanu nisim

וְנִפְלָאוֹת כְּמוֹ שֶׁעָשָׂה
v'nifla-ot k'mo she-asah

לַאֲבוֹתֵינוּ בִּימֵי מַתִּתְיָהוּ וּבָנָיו.
la-avoteinu bimei Matityahu u-vanav.

May the Merciful grant us the miracle of deliverance as
God did for our ancestors in the days of Mattathias and his sons.

בפורים: On *Purim*:

הָרַחֲמָן, הוּא יַעֲשֶׂה לָנוּ נִסִּים
Harachaman hu ya-aseh lanu nisim

וְנִפְלָאוֹת כְּמוֹ שֶׁעָשָׂה
v'nifla-ot k'mo she-asah la-avoteinu

לַאֲבוֹתֵנוּ בִּימֵי מָרְדְּכַי וְאֶסְתֵּר.
bimei Mordechai v'Ester.

May the Merciful grant us the miracle of deliverance as God did for our
ancestors in the days of Mordecai and Esther.

ביום העצמאות: On *Yom Haatzmaut*:

הָרַחֲמָן, הוּא יַעֲשֶׂה לָנוּ נִסִּים
Harachaman hu ya-aseh lanu nisim

וְנִפְלָאוֹת כְּמוֹ שֶׁעָשָׂה לְעַמֵּנוּ
v'nifla-ot k'mo she-asah l'ameinu

בִּימֵי הֲשָׁבַת בָּנִים לִגְבוּלָם.
bimei hashavat banim ligvulam.

May the Merciful grant us the miracle of deliverance as
God did for our people when God restored them to the land of Israel.

הָרַחֲמָן, הוּא יְבָרֵךְ אֶת־אַחֵינוּ
Harachaman hu y'vareich et acheinu

בְּנֵי יִשְׂרָאֵל הַנְּתוּנִים בְּצָרָה,
b'nei Yisrael han'tunim b'tzarah,

וְיוֹצִיאֵם מֵאֲפֵלָה לְאוֹרָה.
v'yotzi'eim mei-afeilah l'orah.

May the Merciful bless all of our people who suffer and bring them out of
darkness into light.

הָרַחֲמָן, הוּא יְבָרֵךְ אֶת־מְדִינַת
Harachaman hu y'vareich et Medinat

יִשְׂרָאֵל, רֵאשִׁית צְמִיחַת גְּאֻלָּתֵנוּ.
Yisrael, reishit tz'michat g'ulateinu.

May the Merciful bless the State of Israel, the dawn of our redemption.

וְנִשָּׂא בְרָכָה מֵאֵת יי, וּצְדָקָה
מֵאֱלֹהֵי יִשְׁעֵנוּ, וְנִמְצָא חֵן
וְשֵׂכֶל טוֹב בְּעֵינֵי אֱלֹהִים וְאָדָם.
עֹשֶׂה שָׁלוֹם בִּמְרוֹמָיו, הוּא
יַעֲשֶׂה שָׁלוֹם עָלֵינוּ וְעַל
כָּל־יִשְׂרָאֵל, וְאִמְרוּ אָמֵן.

V'nisa v'racha me-eit Adonai, utz-daka
mei-Elohei yish-einu, v'nimtza chein
v'seichel tov b'einei Elohim v'adam.
Oseh shalom bimromav hu
ya-aseh shalom aleinu v'al
Kol Yisrael, v'imru amein.

May we receive blessings from the Lord, lovingkindness from the God of our deliverance. May we find grace and good favor before God and all people. May God who brings peace to God's universe bring peace to us, to all the people Israel and to all humankind. And let us say: Amen.

ברכה אחרונה B'RACHA ACHARONA

After cake, wine or certain fruits:

בָּרוּךְ אַתָּה יי אֱלֹהֵינוּ
מֶלֶךְ הָעוֹלָם,

Baruch atah Adonai Eloheinu
Melech ha-olam-

אחרי עוגות:
עַל הַמִּחְיָה וְעַל הַכַּלְכָּלָה,

After cake:
Al hamichya v'al hakalkala,

אחרי היין:
עַל הַגֶּפֶן וְעַל פְּרִי הַגֶּפֶן,

After wine:
Al hagefen v'al p'ri hagefen,

אחרי עוגות ועל היין:
עַל הַמִּחְיָה וְעַל הַכַּלְכָּלָה
וְעַל הַגֶּפֶן וְעַל פְּרִי הַגֶּפֶן

After cake and wine:
Al hamichya v'al hakalkala
v'al hagefen v'al p'ri hagefen,

**אחרי פירות
משבעת המינים:**
עַל הָעֵץ וְעַל פְּרִי הָעֵץ,

*After certain fruits
(of the Seven Species):*
Al ha-eitz v'al p'ri ha-eitz,

וְעַל תְּנוּבַת הַשָּׂדֶה, וְעַל אֶרֶץ
חֶמְדָּה טוֹבָה וּרְחָבָה, שֶׁרָצִיתָ
וְהִנְחַלְתָּ לַאֲבוֹתֵינוּ, לֶאֱכוֹל
מִפִּרְיָהּ וְלִשְׂבּוֹעַ מִטּוּבָהּ. רַחֵם
יְיָ אֱלֹהֵינוּ, עַל יִשְׂרָאֵל עַמֶּךָ,
וְעַל יְרוּשָׁלַיִם עִירֶךָ, וְעַל צִיּוֹן
מִשְׁכַּן כְּבוֹדֶךָ, וְעַל מִזְבְּחַךָ
וְעַל הֵיכָלֶךָ. וּבְנֵה יְרוּשָׁלַיִם
עִיר הַקֹּדֶשׁ בִּמְהֵרָה בְיָמֵינוּ,
וְהַעֲלֵנוּ לְתוֹכָהּ, וְשַׂמְּחֵנוּ
בְּבִנְיָנָהּ, וְנֹאכַל מִפִּרְיָהּ
וְנִשְׂבַּע מִטּוּבָהּ, וּנְבָרֶכְךָ עָלֶיהָ
בִּקְדֻשָּׁה וּבְטָהֳרָה.

V'al t'nuvat hasadeh, v'al eretz
chemda tova ur-chava sheratzita
v'hin-chalta la-avoteinu le-echol
mipirya v'lisbo-a mituva. Rachem
Adonai Eloheinu, al Yisrael amecha,
v'al Y'rushalayim irecha, v'al tziyon
mishkan k'vodecha, v'al mizbachecha,
v'al heichalecha. Uv-nei Y'rushalayim
ir hakodesh bimheira v'yameinu,
v'ha-aleinu l'tochah v'sam'cheinu
b'vinyanah, v'nochal mipiryah
y'nisba mituvah, unvarech'cha aleha
bikdusha uv-tohora.

Praised are You, Lord our God, Sovereign of the universe, for all the
nourishment and produce of the field, for the lovely and spacious land which
You gave to our ancestors as a heritage to eat of its fruit and enjoy its good gifts.
Have mercy, Lord our God, on Your people Israel, on Your city Jerusalem, on
Zion the home of Your majesty, on Your shrine. Speedily rebuild the holy
city of Jerusalem. Bring us there and gladden us with the restoration of our
land. May we eat of its fruit and enjoy its good gifts. May we bless you for it in
holiness and purity.

בשבת: *On Shabbat:*

וּרְצֵה וְהַחֲלִיצֵנוּ בְּיוֹם
הַשַּׁבָּת הַזֶּה.

Ur'tzei v'hachalitzeinu b'yom
haShabbat hazeh.

Be pleased and strengthen us on this Shabbat day.

בראש חודש: On *Rosh Chodesh* say:

וְזָכְרֵנוּ לְטוֹבָה בְּיוֹם V'zochreinu l'tova b'yom
רֹאשׁ הַחֹדֶשׁ הַזֶּה. Rosh Hachodesh hazeh.

Remember us for good on this New Moon.

בראש השנה: On *Rosh Hashanah* say:

וְזָכְרֵנוּ לְטוֹבָה בְּיוֹם V'zochreinu l'tova b'yom
הַזִּכָּרוֹן הַזֶּה. Hazikaron hazeh.

Remember us for good on this Day of Remembrance.

בפסח: On *Pesach* say:

וְשַׂמְּחֵנוּ בְּיוֹם חַג V'sam'cheinu b'yom Chag
הַמַּצּוֹת הַזֶּה. Hamatzot hazeh.

Grant us joy on this festival of Unleavened Bread.

בשבועות: On *Shavu'ot* say:

וְשַׂמְּחֵנוּ בְּיוֹם חַג V'sam'cheinu b'yom Chag
הַשָּׁבֻעוֹת הַזֶּה. Hashavuot hazeh.

Grant us joy on this festival of Weeks.

בסוכות: On *Sukkot* say:

וְשַׂמְּחֵנוּ בְּיוֹם חַג V'sam'cheinu b'yom Chag
הַסֻּכּוֹת הַזֶּה. Hasukkot hazeh.

Grant us joy on this festival of Tabernacles.

בשמע"צ ושמח"ת: On *Sh'mini Atzeret* and *Simchat Torah* say:

וְשַׂמְּחֵנוּ בְּיוֹם הַשְּׁמִינִי V'sam'cheinu bayom hash'mini
חַג הָעֲצֶרֶת הַזֶּה. Chag ha-atzeret hazeh.

Grant us joy on this festival of the Eighth Day of Assembly.

כִּי אַתָּה יי טוב וּמֵטִיב לַכֹּל,
וְנוֹדֶה לְּךָ עַל הָאָרֶץ

Ki ata Adonai tov U'meitiv lakol,
v'nodeh l'cha al ha-aretz

עַל עוּגוֹת:
וְעַל הַמִּחְיָה. בָּרוּךְ אַתָּה יי,
עַל הָאָרֶץ וְעַל הַמִּחְיָה.

After cake:
V'al hamichya. Baruch atah Adonai,
al ha-aretz v'al hamichya.

עַל הַיַּיִן:
וְעַל פְּרִי הַגָּפֶן. בָּרוּךְ אַתָּה יי,
עַל הָאָרֶץ וְעַל פְּרִי הַגָּפֶן.

After wine:
V'al pri hagafen. Baruch ata Adonai,
al ha'aretz v'al pri hagafen.

עַל עוּגוֹת וַיִּין:
וְעַל הַמִּחְיָה וְעַל פְּרִי הַגָּפֶן.
בָּרוּךְ אַתָּה יי, עַל הָאָרֶץ
וְעַל הַמִּחְיָה וְעַל פְּרִי הַגָּפֶן.

After cake and wine:
V'al hamichya v'al p'ri hagafen.
Baruch atah Adonai, al ha-aretz v'al
hamichya v'al p'ri hagafcn.

עַל פֵּירוֹת
מִשִּׁבְעַת הַמִּינִים:
וְעַל הַפֵּרוֹת. בָּרוּךְ אַתָּה יי,
עַל הָאָרֶץ וְעַל הַפֵּרוֹת.

After certain fruits
(of the Seven Species):
V'al haperot. Baruch ata Adonai,
al ha-aretz v'al haperot.

For You, O Lord, are good to all. We thank You for our land and all of the
nourishment. Praised are You, Lord, for the land and the sustenance.

אַחַר שְׁאָר אוֹכְלִין
וּמַשְׁקִין:
בָּרוּךְ אַתָּה יי, אֱלֹהֵינוּ מֶלֶךְ
הָעוֹלָם, בּוֹרֵא נְפָשׁוֹת רַבּוֹת
וְחֶסְרוֹנָן, עַל כָּל מַה שֶׁבָּרָאתָ
לְהַחֲיוֹת בָּהֶם נֶפֶשׁ כָּל חָי.
בָּרוּךְ חֵי הָעוֹלָמִים.

After any food or liquids
requiring the blessing Shehakol:
Baruch atah Adonai Eloheinu Melech
ha-olam, borei n'fashot, rabot
v'chesronan, al kol ma shebarata
l'hachayot bahem nefesh kol chai.
Baruch chei ha-olamim.

Praised are You, Lord our God, Sovereign of the universe, Creator of all life
and its needs, for all things You have created to sustain every living being.
Praised are You, who are the life of the universe.

שִׁירִים קְצָרִים SHIRIM K'TZARIM
(SHORT SONGS)

אַחַת שָׁאַלְתִּי   *Achat sha-alti*

אַחַת שָׁאַלְתִּי מֵאֵת ה'   Achat sha-alti mei-eit Adonai

אוֹתָהּ אֲבַקֵּשׁ: שִׁבְתִּי בְּבֵית־ה'   ota avakeish: shivti b'veit Adonai,

כָּל־יְמֵי חַיַּי,   kol y'mei chayai,

לַחֲזוֹת בְּנֹעַם־ה',   lachazot b'noam hashem,

וּלְבַקֵּר בְּהֵיכָלוֹ.   ul-vaker b'heichalo.

תהילים כז:ד   Psalms 27:4

One thing I ask from the Lord, one thing I desire,
That I may dwell in the house of the Lord all the days of my life.
To embrace the graciousness of the Lord,
And to enter the Lord's sanctuary.

אַחֵינוּ   *Acheinu*

אַחֵינוּ כָּל־בֵּית יִשְׂרָאֵל   Acheinu kol beit Yisrael,

הַנְּתוּנִים בְּצָרָה וּבְשִׁבְיָה,   han'tunim b'tzara uvshivya,

הָעוֹמְדִים בֵּין בַּיָּם   ha-omdim bein bayam

וּבֵין בַּיַּבָּשָׁה,   u-vein baya-basha,

הַמָּקוֹם יְרַחֵם עֲלֵיהֶם   hamakom y'racheim aleihem,

וְיוֹצִיאֵם מִצָּרָה לִרְוָחָה,   v'yotzieim mitzara lirvacha,

וּמֵאֲפֵלָה לְאוֹרָה,   u-mei-afei-la l'ora,

וּמִשִּׁעְבּוּד לִגְאֻלָּה,   u-mishibud ligula,

הַשְׁתָּא בַּעֲגָלָא וּבִזְמַן קָרִיב.   hashta ba-aga-la u-vizman kariv.

שחרית   Weekday Shacharit

May the Holy One be merciful to our fellow Jews who wander over sea and land, who suffer oppression and imprisonment. May God soon bring them relief from distress and deliver them from darkness to light, from subjugation to redemption.

עַל שְׁלֹשָׁה דְבָרִים   Al Sh'losha D'varim

עַל שְׁלֹשָׁה דְּבָרִים

הָעוֹלָם עוֹמֵד:

עַל הַתּוֹרָה וְעַל הָעֲבוֹדָה

וְעַל גְּמִילוּת חֲסָדִים.

פרקי אבות א:ב

Al sh'losha d'varim

ha-olam omeid:

al ha-Torah, v'al ha-avodah

v'al g'milut chasadim.

Pirkei Avot 1:2

The world stands on three things:
On the Torah, on divine service and on deeds of lovingkindness.

עַם יִשְׂרָאֵל חַי   Am Yisrael Chai

עַם יִשְׂרָאֵל חַי! עוֹד אָבִינוּ חַי!

Am Yisrael chai! Od Avinu chai!

The Jewish people lives!
Our Father yet lives!

אָנָּא בְכֹחַ   Ana B'cho'ach

אָנָּא בְּכֹחַ גְּדֻלַת יְמִינְךָ

תַּתִּיר צְרוּרָה. קַבֵּל רִנַּת עַמְּךָ,

שַׂגְּבֵנוּ, טַהֲרֵנוּ, נוֹרָא.

קבלת שבת

Ana b'cho'ach g'dulat y'mincha,

tatir tz'rura. Kabeil rinat amcha

sag-veinu, tahareinu, nora.

Kabbalat Shabbat

We beg You! With the strength of Your right hand's greatness, release Your bound nation. Accept the prayer of Your people; strengthen us, purify us, O awesome one.

79

אני מאמין — Ani Ma-Amin

אֲנִי מַאֲמִין בֶּאֱמוּנָה שְׁלֵמָה
בְּבִיאַת הַמָּשִׁיחַ.
וְאַף־עַל־פִּי שֶׁיִּתְמַהְמֵהַּ,
עִם כָּל־זֶה אֲחַכֶּה לּוֹ
בְּכָל־יוֹם שֶׁיָּבוֹא.

Ani ma-amin be-emunah sh'leima
b'viat ha-mashiach.
v'af al pi she-yitmahmei-a
im kol zeh achakeh lo
b'chol yom sheyavo.

Rambam's 13 Principles of Faith

I believe with perfect faith in the coming of the Messiah, and although the Messiah may tarry, I will wait daily for its coming.

אשר ברא — Asher Bara

אֲשֶׁר בָּרָא שָׂשׂוֹן וְשִׂמְחָה,
חָתָן וְכַלָּה, גִּילָה, רִנָּה, דִּיצָה
וְחֶדְוָה, אַהֲבָה וְאַחֲוָה
וְשָׁלוֹם וְרֵעוּת.

Asher bara sason v'simcha,
chatan v'chalah, gilah, rinah, ditzah
v'chedvah, ahavah v'achavah
v'shalom v'rei-ut.

תלמוד (כתובות ח ע״א)   Talmud Bavli (Ketubot 8a)

God created joy and gladness, bride and groom, mirth, song, delight and rejoicing, love and harmony, peace and companionship.

אשרינו — Ashreinu

אַשְׁרֵינוּ מַה־טּוֹב חֶלְקֵנוּ,
וּמַה נָּעִים גּוֹרָלֵנוּ,
וּמַה־יָּפָה יְרֻשָּׁתֵנוּ.

Ashreinu mah tov chelkeinu,
umah na-im goraleinu
umah yafa y'rushateinu.

תפילת שחרית   Shacharit Service

Happy are we,
How good is our destiny,
How pleasant our lot,
How beautiful our heritage.

אשירה לה׳ · *Ashira Lashem*

אָשִׁירָה לַה׳ בְּחַיָּי,
אֲזַמְּרָה לֵאלֹהַי בְּעוֹדִי.
יֶעֱרַב עָלָיו שִׂיחִי,
אָנֹכִי אֶשְׂמַח בַּה׳.
יִתַּמּוּ חַטָּאִים מִן־הָאָרֶץ
וּרְשָׁעִים עוֹד אֵינָם,
בָּרְכִי נַפְשִׁי אֶת־ה׳, הַלְלוּיָהּ.

Ashira Lashem b'chayai,
azamra lelohai b'odi.
Ye-erav alav sichi,
anochi esmach, Bashem.
vitamu chata'im min ha-aretz
ursha-im od einam,
barchi nafshi et Hashem, Halleluyah.

תהילים קד:לג-לה

Psalms 104:33

I will sing unto the Lord as I live,
I will sing praises to my God while I have any being.
Let my musing be sweet unto him.
As for me I will rejoice in the Lord
Let sinners cease from the earth
And let the wicked be no more,
Bless the Lord, O my soul.

אתה אחד · *Atah Echad*

אַתָּה אֶחָד וְשִׁמְךָ אֶחָד,
וּמִי כְּעַמְּךָ יִשְׂרָאֵל גּוֹי
אֶחָד בָּאָרֶץ. תִּפְאֶרֶת
גְּדֻלָּה, וַעֲטֶרֶת יְשׁוּעָה,
יוֹם מְנוּחָה וּקְדֻשָּׁה
לְעַמְּךָ נָתָתָּ. אַבְרָהָם
יָגֵל, יִצְחָק יְרַנֵּן,
יַעֲקֹב וּבָנָיו יָנוּחוּ בוֹ.

Atah echad v'shimcha echad.
Umi k'amcha Yisrael, goy
echad ba-aretz. Tiferet
g'dulah, va-ateret y'shua,
yom m'nucha uk-dusha
l'amcha natata. Avraham
yageil, Yitzchak y'ranein,
Ya-akov uvanav yanuchu vo.

עמידה לשבת

Shabbat Afternoon Amidah

continued on next page

81

You are One, your name is One,
And who is like your people Israel unique on earth?
A crown of distinction, a crown of salvation,
The Shabbat You gave us for the spirit's rebirth.
Our ancestors have told us that on the Shabbat day,
Abraham and Isaac rejoiced; Jacob and his sons found joy and rest.

אתה הראת   *Atah Horeita*

אַתָּה הָרְאֵתָ לָדַעַת כִּי ה'
הוּא הָאֱלֹהִים, אֵין עוֹד מִלְבַדּוֹ.

Ata horeita lada'at ki Hashem
hu ha'Elohim, ein od milvado.

דברים ד:לה

Deuteronomy 4:35

You have been made to see, to know that Hashem is God. There is none beside God.

ט'שירי בירי בים   *Az Ich Vil Zingen (Chiri Bim)*

אַז אִיךְ וִיל זִינְגֶען:
"לְכָה דוֹדִי"

Az ich vil zingen
"l'cha dodi."

זָאלְסְטוּ זִינְגֶען:
"טְשִׁירִי בִּירִי בִּים"

Zolstu zingen
"chiri biri bim."

אַז אִיךְ וִיל זִינְגֶען:
"לִקְרַאת כַּלָה"

Az ich vil zingen
"likrat kala,"

זָאלְסְטוּ זִינְגֶען:
"טְשִׁירִי בִּירִי בַּאם"

Zolstu zingen
"chiri biri bom."

לְכָה דוֹדִי: טְשִׁירִי בִּירִי בִּים

L'cha dodi: chiri biri bim.

לִקְרַאת כַּלָה: טְשִׁירִי בִּירִי בַּאם

Likrat kala: chiri biri bom.

לְכָה דוֹדִי לִקְרַאת כַּלָה:

L'cha dodi likrat kala,

טְשִׁירִי בִּירִי בִּירִי בִּירִי בִּים

chiri biri biri biri bim.

When I say "L'cha Dodi" you will answer "chiri biri bim."
When I say "Likrat Kala" you will answer "chiri biri bom."

בשם ה' B'sheim Hashem

בְּשֵׁם ה' אֱלֹהֵי יִשְׂרָאֵל,
B'sheim Hashem Elohei Yisrael,

מִימִינִי מִיכָאֵל,
mimini Micha-eil,

וּמִשְּׂמֹאלִי גַּבְרִיאֵל,
u-mismoli Gavri-eil,

וּמִלְּפָנַי אוּרִיאֵל,
u-mil'fanai Uri-eil,

וּמֵאֲחוֹרַי רְפָאֵל,
umei-achorai R'fa'eil,

וְעַל רֹאשִׁי שְׁכִינַת אֵל.
v'al roshi sh'chinat Eil.

קריאת שמע על המטה

Bedtime Shema

In the name of Hashem, God of Israel, may Michael be at my right, Gabriel at my left, before me Uriel, Raphael behind me and above my head, the presence of God.

ברוך אלהינו Baruch Eloheinu

בָּרוּךְ אֱלֹהֵינוּ, שֶׁבְּרָאָנוּ לִכְבוֹדוֹ,
Baruch Eloheinu shebra-anu lichvodo,

וְהִבְדִּילָנוּ מִן הַתּוֹעִים,
v'hivdilanu min hato-im,

וְנָתַן לָנוּ תּוֹרַת אֱמֶת,
V'natan lanu Torat emet,

וְחַיֵּי עוֹלָם נָטַע בְּתוֹכֵנוּ.
v'chayei olam nata b'tocheinu.

תפילת מנחה ליום שבת

Shabbat Mincha

Blessed is our God who has created us for God's glory, and separated us from them that go astray by giving us the Torah of truth, thus planting everlasting life in our midst.

ברוך המקום Baruch Hamakom

בָּרוּךְ הַמָּקוֹם בָּרוּךְ הוּא.
Baruch Hamakom baruch Hu.

בָּרוּךְ שֶׁנָּתַן תּוֹרָה לְעַמּוֹ יִשְׂרָאֵל.
Baruch shenatan Torah l'amo Yisrael.

בָּרוּךְ הוּא.
Baruch Hu.

ההגדה של פסח

Passover Haggadah

Blessed be God, Blessed is God.
Blessed is God who gave the Torah to God's people Israel.
Blessed is God.

בלבבי משכן אבנה | Bilvavi Mishkan Evne

בְּלִבִּי מִשְׁכָּן אֶבְנֶה לַהֲדַר
כְּבוֹדוֹ, וּבַמִּשְׁכָּן מִזְבֵּחַ אָשִׂים
לְקַרְנֵי הוֹדוֹ, וּלְנֵר תָּמִיד
אֶקַּח לִי אֶת־אֵשׁ הָעֲקֵדָה,
וּלְקָרְבָּן אַקְרִיב לוֹ אֶת־נַפְשִׁי
הַיְּחִידָה.

Bilvavi mishkan evne lahadar
k'vodo, u-vamishkan mizbei-ach asim
l'karnei hodo ul'neir tamid
ekach li et eish ha-a-keida,
ul'korban akriv lo et nafshi
ha-y'chida.

אלעזר אזיקרי   Elazar Azikri

In my heart I will build a sanctuary to glorify the honor of God. In the sanctuary I will place an altar to acknowledge the splendor of God. For the eternal light I will take the fire of Isaac's sacrifice, and for a sacrifice, I will offer up to God my unique soul.

דוד מלך ישראל | David Melech Yisrael

דָּוִד מֶלֶךְ יִשְׂרָאֵל חַי וְקַיָּם.

David, Melech Yisrael, chai v'kayam.

David, King of Israel, lives forever.

דודי לי | Dodi Li

דּוֹדִי לִי וַאֲנִי לוֹ
הָרֹעֶה בַּשּׁוֹשַׁנִּים.
מִי זֹאת עֹלָה מִן־הַמִּדְבָּר
מְקֻטֶּרֶת מוֹר וּלְבוֹנָה.

Dodi li va-ani lo
Haro-eh bashoshanim.
Mi zot ola min hamidbar
m'kuteret mor ul-vona.

דּוֹדִי לִי וַאֲנִי לוֹ הָרֹעֶה בַּשּׁוֹשַׁנִּים

Dodi li va-ani lo haro-eh bashoshanim.

לִבַּבְתִּנִי אֲחֹתִי כַלָּה
(לִבַּבְתִּנִי כָלָּה)

Libavtini achoti chala
(Libavtini chala).

דּוֹדִי לִי וַאֲנִי לוֹ הָרֹעֶה בַּשּׁוֹשַׁנִּים

Dodi li va-ani lo haro-eh bashoshanim.

עוּרִי צָפוֹן וּבוֹאִי תֵימָן
(וּבוֹאִי תֵימָן)

Uri tzafon uvo'i teiman
(U'vo'i teiman).

דּוֹדִי לִי וַאֲנִי לוֹ הָרֹעֶה בַּשּׁוֹשַׁנִּים

Dodi li va-ani lo haro-eh bashoshanim.

שיר השירים ב:טז, ג:ו, ד:ט, ד:טז   Song of Songs: 2:16, 3:6, 4:9, 4:16

My beloved is mine and I am his
That feeds among the lilies,
Who is that going up from the wilderness
Burning myrth and incense?
You have ravished my heart
My sister, my bride.

אל ברוך · Eil Baruch

אֵל בָּרוּךְ גְּדוֹל דֵּעָה,	Eil baruch g'dol dei-ah,
הֵכִין וּפָעַל זָהֲרֵי חַמָּה,	heichin u-fa-al zo-ho-rei chama.
טוֹב יָצַר כָּבוֹד לִשְׁמוֹ,	Tov ya-tzar kavod l'shmo,
מְאוֹרוֹת נָתַן סְבִיבוֹת עֻזּוֹ.	m'orot natan s'vivot uzo.
פִּנּוֹת צְבָאָיו קְדוֹשִׁים	Pinot tz'va-av k'doshim
רוֹמְמֵי שַׁדַּי, תָּמִיד	rom'mei Shadai, tamid
מְסַפְּרִים כְּבוֹד אֵל וּקְדֻשָּׁתוֹ.	m'saprim k'vod Eil uk-dushato.

שחרית לחול · Weekday Shacharit

Our praiseworthy God with vast understanding fashioned the rays of the sun. The good light God created reflects the splendor of God; radiant lights surround the throne of God. God's heavenly servants in holiness exalt the almighty, constantly recounting God's sacred glory.

אליך ה' אקרא · Eilecha Hashem Ekra

אֵלֶיךָ ה' אֶקְרָא	Eilecha Hashem ekra
וְאֶל־אֲדֹנָי אֶתְחַנָּן	v'Eil Hashem etchanan,
שְׁמַע־ה' וְחָנֵּנִי,	Sh'ma Hashem v'chaneini
ה' הֱיֵה עֹזֵר לִי	Hashem he-yei ozer li.

תהילים ל:ט, יא · Psalms 30:9, 11

Unto Thee, O God, did I call, and unto the Lord I made supplication, Hear, O God, and be gracious unto me; Lord, be my helper.

85

אלה חמדה לבי   *Eileh Chamda Libi*

אֵלֶּה חָמְדָה לִבִּי,

חוּסָה נָא וְאַל נָא תִּתְעַלֵּם.

Eileh chamda libi,

chusa na v'al na tit-aleim.

These are the desires of my heart.
Have mercy and turn not away from us.

אל ההודאות   *Eil Ha-Hoda-Ot*

אֵל הַהוֹדָאוֹת, אֲדוֹן הַשָּׁלוֹם,

מְקַדֵּשׁ הַשַּׁבָּת

וּמְבָרֵךְ שְׁבִיעִי,

וּמֵנִיחַ בִּקְדֻשָּׁה

לְעַם מְדֻשְּׁנֵי עֹנֶג,

זֵכֶר לְמַעֲשֵׂה בְרֵאשִׁית.

Eil ha-hoda-ot, adon hashalom,

m'kadeish hashabat

um'vareich sh'vi'i,

u-meini-ach bikdusha

l'am m'dushnei oneg,

zeicher l'ma-asei v'reishit.

תפילת מעריב לשבת   Friday night Maariv

God deserving gratitude, the master of peace who hallows Shabbat, in
holiness, granting God's gift of Shabbat to the people thus filled with delight,
recalling the act of creation.

אלי, אלי   *Eili Eili*
(הליכה לקיסריה)   *(Halicha L'keisaria)*

אֵלִי, אֵלִי, שֶׁלֹּא יִגָּמֵר לְעוֹלָם:

הַחוֹל וְהַיָּם,

רִשְׁרוּשׁ שֶׁל הַמַּיִם

בְּרַק הַשָּׁמַיִם, תְּפִלַּת הָאָדָם

Eili, Eili shelo yigameir l'olam:

hachol v'hayam,

rishrush shel hamayim,

b'rak hashamayim, t'filat ha'adam.

Hannah Senesh

Oh Lord, my God, I pray that these things never end: the sand and the sea,
the rush of the waters, the crash of the heavens, the prayer of humankind.

אמת   *Emet*

אֱמֶת, אַתָּה הוּא רִאשׁוֹן

וְאַתָּה הוּא אַחֲרוֹן,

וּמִבַּלְעָדֶיךָ אֵין לָנוּ

מֶלֶךְ גּוֹאֵל וּמוֹשִׁיעַ.

Emet, atah hu rishon

Emet atah hu acharon,

umi-bal-adecha ein lanu

Melech go-eil umoshia.

תפילת שחרית   Shacharit Service

You are the first, You are the last,
And besides You we have no Sovereign or redeemer.

ארץ זבת חלב   *Eretz Zavat Chalav*

אֶרֶץ זָבַת חָלָב וּדְבָשׁ!

Eretz zavat chalav u'd'vash!

דברים כו:ט   Deuteronomy 26:9

A land flowing with milk and honey.

אשא עיני   *Esa Einai*

אֶשָּׂא עֵינַי אֶל־הֶהָרִים,

מֵאַיִן יָבֹא עֶזְרִי.

עֶזְרִי מֵעִם ה',

עֹשֵׂה שָׁמַיִם וָאָרֶץ.

אַל־יִתֵּן לַמּוֹט רַגְלֶךָ,

אַל־יָנוּם שֹׁמְרֶךָ.

הִנֵּה לֹא־יָנוּם וְלֹא יִישָׁן,

שׁוֹמֵר יִשְׂרָאֵל.

ה' שֹׁמְרֶךָ ה' צִלְּךָ

עַל־יַד יְמִינֶךָ.

יוֹמָם הַשֶּׁמֶשׁ לֹא־יַכֶּכָּה

וְיָרֵחַ בַּלָּיְלָה

Esa eina el heharim,

Mei'ayin yavo ezri.

Ezri mei-im Hashem,

Oseh shamayim va-aretz.

Al yitein lamot raglecha,

Al yanum shomrecha.

Hinei lo yanum v'loh yishan,

Shomeir Yisrael.

Hashem shomrecha, adonai tzil'cha

al yad yemincha.

Yomam hashemesh loh ya-ke-ka

Veyareiyach balaila

continued on next page

87

ה' יִשְׁמָרְךָ מִכָּל־רָע	Hashem. Yishmor'cha mikol rah
יִשְׁמֹר אֶת־נַפְשֶׁךָ.	yishmor et nafshecha
ה' יִשְׁמָר־צֵאתְךָ	Hashem yishmor tzatcha
וּבוֹאֶךָ מֵעַתָּה וְעַד־עוֹלָם.	u'vo'echa me'ata v'ad olam.

תהילים קכא:א-ח

Psalms 121:1-8

I will lift my eyes to the hills from where comes my help. My help comes from the Lord who made heaven and earth. The Lord will not let your foot be moved; God who watches you will not slumber. Behold, God who watches Israel shall neither slumber nor sleep.

הַמַּלְאָךְ הַגֹּאֵל — *Hamalach Hagoeil*

הַמַּלְאָךְ הַגֹּאֵל אֹתִי	Hamalach hagoeil oti
מִכָּל־רָע יְבָרֵךְ אֶת־הַנְּעָרִים,	mikol ra y'vareich et ha-n'arim
וְיִקָּרֵא בָהֶם שְׁמִי	v'yikarei vahem sh'mi
וְשֵׁם אֲבֹתַי אַבְרָהָם וְיִצְחָק,	v'sheim avotai Avraham v'Yitzchak
וְיִדְגּוּ לָרֹב בְּקֶרֶב הָאָרֶץ.	v'yidgu larov b'kerev ha-aretz.

בראשית מח:טז

Genesis 48:16

The angel who has redeemed me from all evil, bless the young ones; and let my name be named in them, and the name of my ancestors Abraham and Isaac; and let them grow into a multitude in the midst of the earth.

הָרַחֲמָן — *Harachaman*

הָרַחֲמָן, הוּא יִשְׁלַח לָנוּ	Harachaman, hu yishlach lanu
אֶת אֵלִיָּהוּ הַנָּבִיא,	et Eiliyahu Hanavi
זָכוּר לַטּוֹב, וִיבַשֶּׂר לָנוּ	zachur latov, vivaser lanu
בְּשׂוֹרוֹת טוֹבוֹת יְשׁוּעוֹת וְנֶחָמוֹת.	b'sorot tovot yeshuot v'nechamot.

ברכת המזון

Birkat Hamazon

May the All-Merciful send us Elijah the prophet who shall give us good tidings, salvation, and consolation.

הטוב · Hatov

הַטּוֹב, כִּי לֹא כָלוּ רַחֲמֶיךָ,
וְהַמְרַחֵם,
כִּי לֹא־תַמּוּ חֲסָדֶיךָ,
מֵעוֹלָם קִוְּינוּ לָךְ.

Hatov, ki lo chalu Rachamecha,
V'ham'racheim,
ki lo tamu chasadecha,
mei-olam kivinu lach.

עמידה   Amidah

You who are all-good, whose mercies never fail,
Merciful One, whose kindnesses never cease,
We have hope in you.

הבה נשירה · Hava Nashira

הָבָה נָשִׁירָה שִׁיר. הַלְלוּיָהּ!

Hava nashira shir. Halleluyah!

Let us sing, a song of praise. Praise the Lord!

הנה מה־טוב · Hinei Ma Tov

הִנֵּה מַה־טוֹב וּמַה־נָּעִים
שֶׁבֶת אַחִים גַּם יָחַד.

Hinei ma tov uma na-im
Shevet achim gam yachad.

תהילים קלג:א   Psalms 133:1

Behold, how good and how pleasant it is
For friends to dwell together in unity.

הודו לה' · Hodu Lashem

הוֹדוּ לַה' כִּי טוֹב,
כִּי לְעוֹלָם חַסְדּוֹ.
יֹאמַר נָא יִשְׂרָאֵל,
כִּי לְעוֹלָם חַסְדּוֹ.
יֹאמְרוּ נָא בֵית אַהֲרֹן,
כִּי לְעוֹלָם חַסְדּוֹ.
יֹאמְרוּ נָא יִרְאֵי ה',
כִּי לְעוֹלָם חַסְדּוֹ.

Hodu Lashem ki tov,
ki l'olam chasdo.
Yomar na Yisrael,
ki l'olam chasdo.
Yomru na veit Aharon,
ki l'olam chasdo.
Yomru na ylrei Hashem,
ki l'olam chasdo.

תהילים קיח:א-ד   Psalms 118:1-4

Give thanks to the Lord, for the Lord is good,
For the lovingkindness of the Lord endures forever.
Let Israel say now:
The lovingkindness of the Lord endures forever.
Let now the house of Aaron say:
The lovingkindness of the Lord endures forever.
Let them that revere the Lord say:
The lovingkindness of the Lord endures forever.

הושיעה את עמך   *Hoshia Et Amecha*

הוֹשִׁיעָה אֶת־עַמֶּךָ,

Hoshia et amecha

וּבָרֵךְ אֶת־נַחֲלָתֶךָ,

u'vareich et nachalatecha

וּרְעֵם וְנַשְּׂאֵם עַד־הָעוֹלָם.

u'reim v'nas'eim ad ha-olam.

תהילים כח:ט

Psalms 28:9

Save Your people
And bless Your inheritance;
Tend them and sustain them forever.

אם אשכחך ירושלים   *Im Eshkacheich Y'rushalayim*

אִם־אֶשְׁכָּחֵךְ יְרוּשָׁלָיִם

Im eshkacheich Y'rushalayim

תִּשְׁכַּח יְמִינִי.

tishkach y'mini.

תִּדְבַּק לְשׁוֹנִי לְחִכִּי

Tidbak l'shoni l'chiki

אִם־לֹא אֶזְכְּרֵכִי

im lo ez-k'reichi

אִם־לֹא אַעֲלֶה אֶת־יְרוּשָׁלַיִם

im lo a-aleh et Y'rushalayim

עַל רֹאשׁ שִׂמְחָתִי.

al rosh simchati.

תהילים קלז:ה-ו

Psalms 137:5-6

If I forget you, O Jerusalem, let my right hand forget her cunning. Let my tongue cleave to the roof of my mouth, if I remember you not; if I don't set Jerusalem above my highest joy.

עבדו את־ה' · Ivdu et Hashem

עִבְדוּ אֶת־ה' בְּשִׂמְחָה,
בְּאוּ לְפָנָיו בִּרְנָנָה.

Ivdu et Hashem b'simcha,
bo-u l'fanav birnana.

תהילים ק:ב

Psalms 100:2

Serve the Lord with joy,
come before the Lord with singing.

כי הם חיינו · Ki Heim Chayeinu

כִּי הֵם חַיֵּינוּ וְאֹרֶךְ יָמֵינוּ,
וּבָהֶם נֶהְגֶּה יוֹמָם וָלָיְלָה.

Ki heim chayeinu v'orech yameinu,
u'vahem negeh yomam valaila.

תפילת מעריב

Evening Service

For they are our life and the length of our days;
We will meditate upon them day and night.

כי לא־יטש · Ki Lo Yitosh

כִּי לֹא־יִטֹּשׁ ה' עַמּוֹ,
וְנַחֲלָתוֹ לֹא יַעֲזֹב.
ה' הוֹשִׁיעָה,
הַמֶּלֶךְ יַעֲנֵנוּ בְיוֹם־קָרְאֵנוּ.

Ki lo yitosh Hashem amo,
V'nachalato lo ya-azov.
Hashem hoshia,
Hamelech ya-aneinu v'yom kor-einu.

תהילים צד:יד, כ:י

Psalms 94:14, 20:10

Surely the Lord will not abandon the Lord's people,
nor forsake the heritage of the Lord.
Lord, save us; may the Sovereign answer us when we call.

כי מציון · Ki Mitzion

כִּי מִצִּיּוֹן תֵּצֵא תוֹרָה,
וּדְבַר ה' מִירוּשָׁלָיִם.

Ki Mitzion teitzei Torah,
ud-var Hashem Mirushalayim.

ישעיה ב:ג

(included in Torah Service) Isaiah 2:3

Out of Zion shall come the Torah
And the word of the Lord out of Jerusalem.

כה אמר · Ko Amar

כֹּה אָמַר ה':
מָצָא חֵן בַּמִּדְבָּר
עַם שְׂרִידֵי חָרֶב,
הָלוֹךְ לְהַרְגִּיעוֹ יִשְׂרָאֵל.

ירמיהו לא:א

Ko Amar Hashem:

Matza chein bamidbar

Am s'ridei charev,

haloch l'hargio Yisrael.

Jeremiah 31:1

Thus said the Lord:
The people which were left of the sword
Found grace in the wilderness;
Even Israel, when I went to cause him to rest.

כל העולם כלו · Kol Ha-Olam Kulo

כָּל־הָעוֹלָם כֻּלּוֹ גֶּשֶׁר צַר מְאֹד,
וְהָעִקָּר לֹא לְפַחֵד כְּלָל.

Kol ha-olam kulo gesher tzar m'od,

V'ha-ikar lo l'facheid k'lal.

Rabbi Nachman of Bratslav

The entire world is a narrow bridge,
But the main thing is not to fear.

לכו נרננה · L'chu N'ran'na

לְכוּ נְרַנְּנָה לַה',
נָרִיעָה לְצוּר יִשְׁעֵנוּ.
נְקַדְּמָה פָנָיו בְּתוֹדָה,
בִּזְמִרוֹת נָרִיעַ לוֹ.

קבלת שבת

L'chu n'ran'na lashem,

naria l'tzur yisheinu.

N'kadima fanav b'toda,

bizmirot naria lo.

Friday Night Kabbalat Shabbat Service

O Come, let us sing unto the Lord,
Let us joyfully acclaim the Rock of our salvation.
Let us approach the Lord with thanksgiving,
And acclaim the Lord with songs of praise.

92

למען אחי · L'ma'an Achai

לְמַעַן אַחַי וְרֵעָי
אֲדַבְּרָה נָּא שָׁלוֹם בָּךְ.
לְמַעַן בֵּית ה' אֱלֹהֵינוּ
אֲבַקְשָׁה טוֹב לָךְ.
ה' עֹז לְעַמּוֹ יִתֵּן,
ה' יְבָרֵךְ אֶת־עַמּוֹ בַשָּׁלוֹם.

L'ma'an achai v're'ai
adabra na shalom bach
l'ma'an beit Hashem Eloheinu
avaksha tov lach.
Hashem oz l'amo yitein,
Hashem y'vareich et amo vashalom.

תהילים קכב:ח-ט. כט:יא   Psalms 122:8-9, 29:11

For my brothers and companions' sakes, I will now say, peace be within you.
Because of the house of the Lord our God I will seek your good. The Lord
will give strength to his people; the Lord will bless the Lord's people with
peace.

לשנה הבאה · L'shanah Haba'ah

לְשָׁנָה הַבָּאָה בִּירוּשָׁלָיִם.

L'shanah haba'ah b'Y'rushalayim.

ההגדה של פסח   Passover Haggadah

Next Year in Jerusalem!

למנצח שיר מזמור · Lamnatzeiach Shir Mizmor

לַמְנַצֵּחַ שִׁיר מִזְמוֹר,
הָרִיעוּ לֵאלֹהִים כָּל־הָאָרֶץ.
יָקוּם אֱלֹהִים יָפוּצוּ אוֹיְבָיו,
וְיָנֻסוּ מְשַׂנְאָיו מִפָּנָיו.
לַמְנַצֵּחַ...
לֹא יָנוּם וְלֹא יִישָׁן
שׁוֹמֵר יִשְׂרָאֵל.
לַמְנַצֵּחַ...

Lamnatzeiach shir mizmor,
hari'u l'eilohim kol ha'aretz.
Yakum Elohim yafutzu oy'vav,
v'yanusu m'sna'av mipanav.
   Lamnatzeiach...
Lo, yanum, v'lo yishan,
shomeir Yisrael.
   Lamnatzeiach...

תהילים סו:א. סח:ב. קכא:ד   Psalms 66:1, 68:2, 121:4

93

To the chief musician, a song, a psalm. Raise a shout for God, all the earth. God will arise, God's enemies shall be scattered, God's foes shall flee before him. The guardian of Israel neither sleeps nor slumbers.

לֵב טָהוֹר בְּרָא־לִי Lev Tahor B'rah Li

לֵב טָהוֹר בְּרָא־לִי אֱלֹהִים,
Lev tahor b'rah li Elohim,

וְרוּחַ נָכוֹן חַדֵּשׁ בְּקִרְבִּי.
V'ruach nachon chadeish b'kirbi

אַל־תַּשְׁלִיכֵנִי מִלְּפָנֶיךָ
Al tashlicheini mil'fanecha,

וְרוּחַ קָדְשְׁךָ אַל־תִּקַּח מִמֶּנִּי.
V'ruach kodsh'cha al tikach mimeni.

תהילים נא: יב-יג
Psalms 51:12-14

Create in me a clean heart, O God; and renew a constant spirit inside me.
Do not cast me away from your presence; and do not take your holy spirit from me.
Restore to me the joy of your salvation; and uphold me with a willing spirit.

לֹא עָלֶיךָ Lo Alecha

לֹא עָלֶיךָ הַמְּלָאכָה לִגְמוֹר,
Lo alecha ham'lacha ligmor,

וְלֹא אַתָּה בֶן חוֹרִין
V'lo atah ven chorine

לְהִבָּטֵל מִמֶּנָּה.
L'hibateil mi-menah.

שֶׁיִּבָּנֶה בֵּית הַמִּקְדָּשׁ
She-yibaneh beit hamikdash

בִּמְהֵרָה בְיָמֵינוּ.
Bimheira b'yameinu.

אבות ב:כא
Pirkei Avot 2:21

It is not for you to complete the work,
but neither are you free to desist from it.
May the Temple be speedily rebuilt in our days.

לֹא־אִירָא · Lo Ira

לֹא־אִירָא מֵרִבְבוֹת עָם
אֲשֶׁר סָבִיב, שָׁתוּ עָלָי.
קוּמָה ה' הוֹשִׁיעֵנִי.

Lo ira meriv'vot am
asher saviv shatu alai.
kuma Hashem hoshi-eini.

תהילים ג:ז-ח

Psalms 3:7-8

I will not fear the multitudes
That have set themselves against me.
Arise, Lord! Save me.

לֹא־יִשָּׂא גוֹי · Lo Yisa Goy

לֹא־יִשָּׂא גוֹי אֶל־גּוֹי חֶרֶב
וְלֹא־יִלְמְדוּ עוֹד מִלְחָמָה.

Lo yisa goy el goy cherev
Lo yilm'du od milchama.

ישעיה ב:ד

Isaiah 2:4

Nation shall not lift up sword against nation,
Neither shall they learn war anymore.

מַלְכוּתֶךָ · Malchut'cha

מַלְכוּתְךָ מַלְכוּת כָּל־עֹלָמִים,
וּמֶמְשַׁלְתְּךָ בְּכָל־דּוֹר וָדֹר.

Malchut'cha malchut kol olamim,
umemshalt'cha b'chol dor vador.

תהילים קמה:יג

Psalms 145:13

Your kingdom is an everlasting kingdom
And your dominion will endure throughout all generations.

מַה־טֹּבוּ · Ma Tovu

מַה־טֹּבוּ אֹהָלֶיךָ, יַעֲקֹב
מִשְׁכְּנֹתֶיךָ יִשְׂרָאֵל.

Ma tovu ohalecha Ya-akov
Mishk'notecha Yisrael.

שחרית
במדבר כד:ה

Shacharit Service
Numbers 24:5

How goodly are your tents, O Jacob, your dwelling places, O Israel.

95

מים Mayim

וּשְׁאַבְתֶּם־מַיִם בְּשָׂשׂוֹן
מִמַּעַיְנֵי הַיְשׁוּעָה.

U'shavtem mayim b'sason
Mima-aynei ha-y'shua.

ישעיה יב:ג | Isaiah 12:3

Joyfully shall you draw upon the fountains of deliverance.

מִי־הָאִישׁ Mi Ha-ish

מִי־הָאִישׁ הֶחָפֵץ חַיִּים,
אֹהֵב יָמִים לִרְאוֹת טוֹב.
נְצֹר לְשׁוֹנְךָ מֵרָע,
וּשְׂפָתֶיךָ מִדַּבֵּר מִרְמָה.
סוּר מֵרָע וַעֲשֵׂה־טוֹב,
בַּקֵּשׁ שָׁלוֹם וְרָדְפֵהוּ.

Mi ha-ish he-chafeitz chayim,
Oheiv yamim lir-ot tov.
N'tzor l'shon-cha mei-ra,
Us-fatecha mi-dabeir mirma.
Sur mei-rah v'oseh tov,
bakeish shalom v'rodfehu.

תהילים לד:יג-טו | Psalms 34:13-15

Who is the person that desires life and loves a long life of happiness?

Keep your tongue from evil and your lips from speaking falsehood. Shun evil and do good, seek peace and pursue it.

מִן־הַמֵּצַר Min Hameitzar

מִן־הַמֵּצַר קָרָאתִי יָּהּ,
עָנָנִי בַמֶּרְחָב יָהּ.

Min hameitzar karati Ya.
Anani vamerchav Ya.

תהילים קיח:ה (הלל) | Psalms 118:5 (Hallel)

Out of distress I called upon the Lord. God answered me and set me free.

מִצְוָה גְדוֹלָה   Mitzvah G'dola

מִצְוָה גְדוֹלָה לִהְיוֹת
בְּשִׂמְחָה תָּמִיד.
שִׂמְחָה גְדוֹלָה לִהְיוֹת
בְּמִצְוָה תָּמִיד.

Mitzva g'dola lihiyot
b'simcha tamid.
Simcha g'dola lihiyot
b'mitzvah tamid.

Rabbi Nachman of Bratzlav

It is a great mitzvah to always be happy. It is a joy to always do miztvot.

נַחֲמוּ   Nachamu

נַחֲמוּ נַחֲמוּ עַמִּי,
יֹאמַר אֱלֹהֵיכֶם.
דַּבְּרוּ עַל־לֵב יְרוּשָׁלַיִם
וְקִרְאוּ אֵלֶיהָ כִּי מָלְאָה צְבָאָהּ
כִּי נִרְצָה עֲוֹנָהּ,
כִּי לָקְחָה מִיַּד ה׳
כִּפְלַיִם בְּכָל־חַטֹּאתֶיהָ.
קוֹל קוֹרֵא בַּמִּדְבָּר
פַּנּוּ דֶּרֶךְ ה׳,
יַשְּׁרוּ בָּעֲרָבָה מְסִלָּה לֵאלֹהֵינוּ.

Nachamu, nachamu ami,
yomar Eloheichem.
Dabru al leiv Y'rushalayim
v'kiru ei-leha ki mal'a tz'va-a
ki nirtza avona,
ki lakcha miyad Hashem
kif-layim b'chol chatoteha.
Kol korei bamidbar
panu derech Hashem,
yashru ba-arava m'sila L'Eiloheinu.

ישעיה מ:א-ג   Isaiah 40:1-3

Comfort oh comfort My people, says your God. Speak tenderly to Jerusalem, and declare to her that her time of service is accomplished, that her iniquity is paid off; that she has received at the hand of the Lord double for all her sins. A voice calls out: Clear in the wilderness a road for the Lord. Level in the wilderness a highway for our God! Let every valley be raised, every hill and mount made low.

97

עוֹד יִשָּׁמַע   Od Yishama

עוֹד יִשָּׁמַע בְּעָרֵי יְהוּדָה
וּבְחוּצוֹת יְרוּשָׁלָיִם,
קוֹל שָׂשׂוֹן וְקוֹל שִׂמְחָה,
קוֹל חָתָן וְקוֹל כַּלָּה.

Od yishama b'arei Y'huda
u-v'chutzot Y'rushalayim,
kol sasson v'kol simcha,
kol chatan v'kol kalah.

ירמיה לג:י-יא   Jeremiah 33:10-11

Again may these be heard in the cities of Judah
And in the streets of Jerusalem
The voice of gladness and the voice of happiness
The voice of bridegroom and bride.

אוֹר זָרֻעַ   Or Zarua

אוֹר זָרֻעַ לַצַּדִּיק,
וּלְיִשְׁרֵי-לֵב שִׂמְחָה.

Or zarua latzadik,
Ul-yishrei lev simcha.

תהילים צז:יא   Psalms 97:11

Light is sown for the righteous
And joy for the upright in heart.

עוֹשֶׂה שָׁלוֹם   Oseh Shalom

עוֹשֶׂה שָׁלוֹם בִּמְרוֹמָיו,
הוּא יַעֲשֶׂה שָׁלוֹם עָלֵינוּ,
וְעַל כָּל יִשְׂרָאֵל, וְאִמְרוּ אָמֵן.

Oseh shalom bimromav,
Hu ya-aseh shalom aleinu,
v'al kol Yisrael, v'imru Amein.

קדיש   Kaddish

May God who makes peace in the high places
 make peace for us and for all the people of Israel, and say Amen.

פתחו־לי *Pitchu Li*

פִּתְחוּ־לִי שַׁעֲרֵי־צֶדֶק,
אָבֹא־בָם אוֹדֶה יָהּ.
זֶה־הַשַּׁעַר לַה'
צַדִּיקִים יָבֹאוּ בוֹ.

Pit-chu li sha-arei tzedek
avo vam odeh Yah.
Zeh hasha'ar lashem
tzadikim yavo'u vo.

תהילים קיח:יט-כ

Psalms 118:19

Open to me the gates of righteousness;
I will enter them and give thanks to the Lord.

רוממו *Rom'mu*

רוֹמְמוּ ה' אֱלֹהֵינוּ,
וְהִשְׁתַּחֲווּ לְהַר קָדְשׁוֹ.
כִּי־קָדוֹשׁ ה' אֱלֹהֵינוּ.

Rom'mu Hashem Eloheinu,
v'hishtachavu l'har kodsho.
Ki kadosh Hashem Eloheinu rom'mu.

תהילים צט:ט

Psalms 99:9

Exalt the Lord our God
and worship at the holy mountain of the Lord,
for the Lord our God is holy.

שלום רב *Shalom Rav*

שָׁלוֹם רָב עַל יִשְׂרָאֵל עַמְּךָ
תָּשִׂים לְעוֹלָם, כִּי אַתָּה הוּא
מֶלֶךְ אָדוֹן לְכָל הַשָּׁלוֹם.
וְטוֹב בְּעֵינֶיךָ לְבָרֵךְ אֶת עַמְּךָ
יִשְׂרָאֵל בְּכָל עֵת וּבְכָל שָׁעָה
בִּשְׁלוֹמֶךָ.

Shalom Rav al Yisrael amcha
tasim l'olam, ki Atah hu
melech adon l'chol ha'shalom.
V'tov b'eineicha l'varech et amcha
Yisrael b'chol et uv'chol sha'ah
bishlomecha.

עמידה למנחה ולמעריב

Mincha/Maariv Amidah

Grant true and lasting peace to your people Israel and to all who dwell on earth, for you are the Supreme Sovereign of peace. May it please You to bless Your people Israel in every season and at all times with your gift of peace.

סִמָן טוֹב Siman Tov

סִמָן טוֹב וּמַזָל טוֹב Siman tov u-mazal tov
יְהֵא לָנוּ וּלְכָל־יִשְׂרָאֵל y'hei lanu ul'chol Yisrael.

Kiddush HaLevanah Service

A good sign, good fortune for us and for all of Israel.

תן שבת ותן שלום Tein Shabbat V'tein Shalom

הַצְלָלִים כְּבָר מִתְאָרְכִים Hatz'lalim k'var mit-archim
אַחַר הַצָּהֳרַיִם achar hatzohorayim
תֵּן שַׁבָּת וְתֵן שָׁלוֹם tein Shabbat v'tein shalom
בָּעִיר יְרוּשָׁלָיִם. ba'ir Y'rushalayim.

וְתֵן לָנוּ שְׁעַת מַלְכוּת V'tein lanu sh'at malchut
כָּזֹאת שֶׁבֵּין עַרְבַּיִם kazot shel bein arbayim
תֵּן שָׁלוֹם וְתֵן שַׁבָּת tein shalom v'tein Shabbat
בָּעִיר יְרוּשָׁלָיִם. ba'ir Y'rushalayim.

תֵּן שַׁבָּת וְתֵן שָׁלוֹם Tein Shabbat v'tein shalom
בָּעִיר יְרוּשָׁלַיִם ba'ir Y'rushalayim
תֵּן שָׁלוֹם וְתֵן שַׁבָּת v'tein shalom v'tein Shabbat
בָּעִיר יְרוּשָׁלָיִם... ba'ir Y'rushalayim.

הִנֵּה בָּאָה הַשַּׁבָּת Hinei ba-ah hashabbat im
עִם סֹמֶק הַשָּׁמַיִם somek hashamayim
תֵּן שַׁבָּת וְתֵן שָׁלוֹם tein Shabbat v'tein shalom
בָּעִיר יְרוּשָׁלָיִם. ba'ir Y'rushalayim.

הִנֵּה שָׁלוֹם יוֹרֵד עָלַי Hinei shalom yoreid alai
יוֹרֵד בִּצְחוֹר כְּנָפַיִם yoreid bitz-chor k'nafayim
תֵּן שָׁלוֹם וְתֵן שַׁבָּת tein shalom v'tein Shabbat
בָּעִיר יְרוּשָׁלָיִם. ba'ir Y'rushalayim.

תֵּן שַׁבָּת וְתֵן שָׁלוֹם... *Tein Shabbat...*

כָּל־הַמִּגְדָּלִים כֻּלָּם
מִשְׁתַּחֲוִים אַפַּיִם
תֵּן שַׁבָּת וְתֵן שָׁלוֹם
בָּעִיר יְרוּשָׁלָיִם.

Kol hamigdalim kulam
mishtachavim apayim
tein Shabbat v'tein shalom
ba'ir Y'rushalayim.

אוֹר גָּדוֹל הִנֵּה נִדְלַק
בְּאִישׁוֹנֵי עֵינַיִם
תֵּן שַׁבָּת וְתֵן שָׁלוֹם
בָּעִיר יְרוּשָׁלָיִם.

Or gadol hinei nidlak
b'i-shonei einayim
tein shalom v'tein Shabbat
ba'ir Y'rushalayim.

תֵּן שַׁבָּת וְתֵן שָׁלוֹם...

Tein Shabbat...

Lyrics: Haim Hefer, Music: Dov Seltzer
Copyright © April Music Ltd., Israel

The afternoon shadows have grown longer. Behold peace descends on the approaching Shabbat. Grant Shabbat rest and peace in Jerusalem.

טוב להדות   *Tov L'hodot*

טוֹב לְהֹדוֹת לַה',
וּלְזַמֵּר לְשִׁמְךָ עֶלְיוֹן.
לְהַגִּיד בַּבֹּקֶר חַסְדֶּךָ,
וֶאֱמוּנָתְךָ בַּלֵּילוֹת.

Tov l'hodot lashem,
ul-zamer l'shimcha el-yon.
L'hagid baboker chasdecha,
ve-emunat'cha baleilot.

תהילים צב:ב-ג

Psalms 92:2-3

It is good to give thanks to the Lord,
and to sing praises to Your name, O Most High.
To proclaim Your goodness in the morning
and Your faithfulness at night.

צדיק כתמר   *Tzadik Katamar*

צַדִּיק כַּתָּמָר יִפְרָח,
Tzadik katamar yifrach,

כְּאֶרֶז בַּלְּבָנוֹן יִשְׂגֶּה.
K'erez balvanon yisgeh.

שְׁתוּלִים בְּבֵית ה',
Sh'tulim b'veit Hashem,

בְּחַצְרוֹת אֱלֹהֵינוּ יַפְרִיחוּ.
b'chatzrot Eloheinu yafrichu.

עוֹד יְנוּבוּן בְּשֵׂיבָה,
Od y'nuvun b'seiva,

דְּשֵׁנִים וְרַעֲנַנִּים יִהְיוּ.
d'sheinim v'ra'nanim yihyu.

לְהַגִּיד כִּי־יָשָׁר ה',
L'hagid ki yashar Hashem,

צוּרִי וְלֹא־עַוְלָתָה בּוֹ.
tzuri v'lo avlata bo.

תהילים צב:יג-טז   Psalms 92:13-16

The righteous shall flourish like the palm tree, And grow mighty like a cedar in Lebanon. They shall still bring forth fruit in old age; they shall be fat and flourishing; To declare that the Lord is upright; the Lord is my rock, and there is no unrighteousness in the Lord.

ציון   *Tzion*

צִיּוֹן הֲלֹא תִשְׁאֲלִי
Tzion ha-lo tish-ali

לִשְׁלוֹם אֲסִירָיִךְ.
lishlom asira-yich.

רבי יהודה הלוי   Yehuda Halevi

O Zion, will you not inquire after the well-being of your captive exiles?

ופרצת   *U'faratzta*

וּפָרַצְתָּ יָמָּה וָקֵדְמָה
U'faratzta yama vakeidma

וְצָפֹנָה וָנֶגְבָּה.
tzafona vanegba.

בראשית כח:יד   Genesis 28:14

And You shall spread forth
To the west, to the east, to the north and to the south.

עורה כבודי   U'ra Ch'vodi

עוּרָה כְבוֹדִי עוּרָה הַנֵּבֶל
וְכִנּוֹר אָעִירָה שָּׁחַר.

Ura ch'vodi, ura haneivel
v'chinor a-ira shachar.

תהילים נז:ט   Psalms 57:9

Awake my glory;
Awake psaltery and harp,
I will awaken the dawn.

וראה־בנים   Ur'ei Vanim

וּרְאֵה־בָנִים לְבָנֶיךָ,
שָׁלוֹם עַל־יִשְׂרָאֵל

Ur-ei vanim l'vanecha,
shalom al Yisrael.

תהילים קכח:ו   Psalms 128:6

May you live to see your children's children.
Peace be upon Israel.

ובאו האבדים   U'va'u Ha'ov'dim

וּבָאוּ הָאֹבְדִים בְּאֶרֶץ אַשּׁוּר,
וְהַנִּדָּחִים בְּאֶרֶץ מִצְרָיִם,
וְהִשְׁתַּחֲווּ לַה' בְּהַר
הַקֹּדֶשׁ בִּירוּשָׁלָיִם.

U'va'u ha'ov'dim b'eretz Ashur,
v'hanidachim b'eretz Mitzrayim,
v'hishtachavu Lashem b'har
hakodesh Birushalayim.

ישעיה כז:יג   Isaiah 27:13

Those who were lost in the land of Assyria,
And those who were cast away in the land of Egypt,
Shall come and worship the Lord on the holy mountain at Jerusalem.

וְעֵינֵינוּ תִרְאֶינָה   *V'Eineinu Tir-ena*

וְעֵינֵינוּ תִרְאֶינָה מַלְכוּתֶךָ,

V'eineinu tir-ena malchutecha,

כַּדָּבָר הָאָמוּר בְּשִׁירֵי עֻזֶּךָ,

kadavar ha-amur b'shirei uzecha,

עַל יְדֵי דָּוִד מְשִׁיחַ צִדְקֶךָ.

al y'dei David m'shiach tzidkecha.

עמידה לשחרית של שבת

Shabbat Shacharit Amidah

May our eyes behold the establishment of Your kingdom,
According to the word that was spoken in the Psalms
By David, Your righteous annointed.

וְהָאֵר עֵינֵינוּ   *V'ha-eir Eineinu*

וְהָאֵר עֵינֵינוּ בְּתוֹרָתֶךָ,

V'ha-eir eineinu b'toratecha,

וְדַבֵּק לִבֵּנוּ בְּמִצְוֹתֶיךָ,

v'dabeik libeinu b'mitzvotecha,

וְיַחֵד לְבָבֵנוּ

V'yacheid l'vaveinu

לְאַהֲבָה וּלְיִרְאָה אֶת שְׁמֶךָ.

l'ahava ul-yira et sh'mecha,

וְלֹא נֵבוֹשׁ וְלֹא נִכָּלֵם

v'lo neivosh v'lo nikaleim

וְלֹא נִכָּשֵׁל לְעוֹלָם וָעֶד.

v'lo nikashel l'olam va-ed.

תפילת שחרית

Shacharit Service

Enlighten our eyes in Your Torah;
Attach our heart to Your commandments;
Unite our heart to love and revere Your name,
So that we may never be put to shame.

וְקָרֵב פְּזוּרֵינוּ   *V'kareiv P'zureinu*

וְקָרֵב פְּזוּרֵינוּ מִבֵּין הַגּוֹיִם,

V'kareiv p'zureinu mibein hagoyim,

וּנְפוּצוֹתֵינוּ כַּנֵּס מִיַּרְכְּתֵי־אָרֶץ.

u'n'futzoteinu kaneis mi-yark'tei aretz.

עמידה של מוסף
לשלוש רגלים ולימים נוראים

Festival Musaf Amidah

Unite our scattered people from among the nations, and gather our dispersed from the ends of the earth.

ונאמר לפניו · V'nomar L'fanav

וְנֹאמַר לְפָנָיו שִׁירָה חֲדָשָׁה.
הַלְלוּיָהּ.

V'nomar l'fanav shira chadasha,
Halleluyah.

הגדה של פסח

The Passover Haggadah

Let us recite before Him a new song.
Praise the Lord.

וטהר לבנו · V'taheir Libeinu

וְטַהֵר לִבֵּנוּ לְעָבְדְּךָ בֶּאֱמֶת.

V'taheir libeinu l'ovd'cha be-emet.

עמידה לשבת וליום טוב

Amidah for Shabbat and Festivals

Purify our hearts to serve You sincerely.

יהי־שלום בחילך · Y'hi Shalom B'cheileich

יְהִי־שָׁלוֹם בְּחֵילֵךְ,
שַׁלְוָה בְּאַרְמְנוֹתָיִךְ.

Y'hi shalom b'cheileich
shalva b'ar-m'notayich.

תהלים קכב:ז

Psalms 122:7

May there be peace be within your walls, serenity within your homes.

יברכך · Y'varech'cha

יְבָרֶכְךָ ה' מִצִּיּוֹן,
וּרְאֵה בְּטוּב יְרוּשָׁלָיִם.
כֹּל יְמֵי חַיֶּיךָ.
וּרְאֵה־בָנִים לְבָנֶיךָ,
שָׁלוֹם עַל־יִשְׂרָאֵל.

Y'varech'cha Hashem mi-Tzion
ur-ei b'tuv Y'rushalayim.
kol y'mei chayecha.
Ur-ei vanim l'vanecha,
shalom al Yisrael.

תהילים קכח:ה-ו

Psalms 128:5-6

The Lord will bless you out of Zion
And see the good of Jerusalem.
The Lord will bless you out of Zion
All the days of your life.
May you live to see your children's children.
Peace be upon Israel.

105

יָשִׂישׂ עָלַיִךְ — Yasis Alayich

יָשִׂישׂ עָלַיִךְ אֱלֹהָיִךְ
כִּמְשׂוֹשׂ חָתָן עַל־כַּלָּה.

שלמה אלקבץ (לכה דודי)

Yasis alayich Elohayich
kimsos chatan al kala.

Shlomo Alkabetz,
16th century Kabbalist (Lecha Dodi)

Your God shall rejoice over you
As a bridegroom rejoice over his bride.

יבנה המקדש — Yibaneh Hamikdash

יִבָּנֶה הַמִּקְדָּשׁ,
עִיר צִיּוֹן תְּמַלֵּא,
וְשָׁם נָשִׁיר שִׁיר חָדָשׁ,
וּבִרְנָנָה נַעֲלֶה.

צור משלו
(זמירות לליל שבת)

Yibaneh hamikdash,
ir Tzion timalei,
v'sham nashir shir chadash,
u-vir'nana na-aleh.

Tzur Mishelo
(song for Friday night)

The Temple will be rebuilt,
The city of Zion will be filled.
And there we will sing a new song
and be uplifted with rejoicing.

ישמחו במלכותך — Yism'chu B'mal'chut'cha

יִשְׂמְחוּ בְמַלְכוּתְךָ
שׁוֹמְרֵי שַׁבָּת וְקוֹרְאֵי עֹנֶג.
עַם מְקַדְּשֵׁי שְׁבִיעִי,
כֻּלָּם יִשְׂבְּעוּ וְיִתְעַנְּגוּ מִטּוּבֶךָ.
וְהַשְּׁבִיעִי רָצִיתָ בּוֹ וְקִדַּשְׁתּוֹ.
חֶמְדַּת יָמִים אוֹתוֹ קָרָאתָ,
זֵכֶר לְמַעֲשֵׂה בְרֵאשִׁית.

מוסף לשבת

Yism-chu b'mal'chut'cha
shom'rei Shabbat v'kor'ei oneg.
Am m'kad'shei shi'vi-i,
kulam yisb'u v'yit-an'gu mituvecha
v'ha'shvi'i ratzita bo v'kidashto.
Chemdat yamim oto karata
zeicher l'ma-asei v'reishit.

Shabbat Musaf

May they who observe Shabbat and call it a delight rejoice in Your Kingdom. May the people who sanctify the seventh day be satisfied and delighted. For You did find pleasure in the seventh day, and did sanctify it, calling it the most desirable of days, in remembrance of creation.

ישמחו השמים   *Yism'chu Hashamayim*

יִשְׂמְחוּ הַשָּׁמַיִם   Yism'chu hashamayim

וְתָגֵל הָאָרֶץ,   v'tagel ha-aretz,

יִרְעַם הַיָּם וּמְלֹאוֹ.   yir-am hayam um-lo-o.

תהילים צו:יא   Psalms 96:11

Let the heavens rejoice, let the earth be glad;
Let the sea roar, and all within it give praise.

שירי ארץ ישראל SONGS OF ISRAEL

Israeli music began with the waves of aliyah to Israel. It took on characteristics of the music of the countries from which the immigrant composers came. As more and more composers are native to Israel, their music reflects life in Israel today.

Permission to use the English translations was received from the American Zionist Youth Foundation, Education Department.

על כל-אלה Al Kol Eileh

Lyrics and Music: Naomi Shemer

עַל הַדְּבַשׁ וְעַל הָעֹקֶץ,
Al had'vash v'al ha-oketz,

עַל הַמַּר וְהַמָּתוֹק,
Al hamar v'hamatok,

עַל בִּתֵּנוּ הַתִּינֹקֶת,
Al biteinu hatinoket,

שְׁמֹר אֵלִי הַטּוֹב.
Sh'mor eili hatov.

עַל הָאֵשׁ הַמְבֹעֶרֶת,
Al ha-eish ham'vo-eret,

עַל הַמַּיִם הַזַּכִּים,
Al hamayim hazakim,

עַל הָאִישׁ הַשָּׁב הַבַּיְתָה
Al ha-ish hashav habaita

מִן הַמֶּרְחַקִּים.
Min hamerchakim.

עַל כָּל אֵלֶּה, עַל כָּל אֵלֶּה,
Al kol eileh, al kol eileh,

שְׁמֹר נָא לִי, אֵלִי הַטּוֹב.
Sh'mor na li, eili hatov.

עַל הַדְּבַשׁ וְעַל הָעֹקֶץ,
Al had'vash v'al ha-oketz,

עַל הַמַּר וְהַמָּתוֹק.
Al hamar v'hamatok.

אַל-נָא תַּעֲקֹר נָטוּעַ,
Al na ta-akor natu-a,

אַל תִּשְׁכַּח אֶת הַתִּקְוָה,
Al tishkach et hatikva.

הֲשִׁיבֵנִי וְאָשׁוּבָה,
Hashiveini v'ashuva,

אֶל הָאָרֶץ הַטּוֹבָה.
El ha-aretz hatova.

108

<table>
<tr><td align="right">

שְׁמֹר אֵלִי עַל זֶה הַבַּיִת,
עַל הַגַּן, עַל הַחוֹמָה,
מִיָּגוֹן, מִפַּחַד־פֶּתַע
וּמִמִּלְחָמָה.

</td><td>

Sh'mor eili al zeh habayit,
Al hagan al hachoma,
Miyagon, mipachad peta
umimilchama.

</td></tr>
<tr><td align="right">

שְׁמֹר עַל הַמְּעַט שֶׁיֵּשׁ לִי,
עַל הָאוֹר וְעַל הַטַּף,
עַל הַפְּרִי שֶׁלֹּא הִבְשִׁיל עוֹד
וְשֶׁנֶּאֱסַף.
עַל כָּל אֵלֶּה...

</td><td>

Sh'mor al ham'at she-yeish li,
Al ha-or v'al hataf,
Al hapri shelo hivshil od
V'she-ne-e-saf.
Al kol eileh...

</td></tr>
<tr><td align="right">

מְרַשְׁרֵשׁ אִילָן בָּרוּחַ,
מֵרָחוֹק נוֹשֵׁר כּוֹכָב,
מִשְׁאֲלוֹת לִבִּי בַּחֹשֶׁךְ,
נִרְשָׁמוֹת עַכְשָׁיו.

</td><td>

Merashresh ilan baru'ach,
merachok nosher kochav,
mish'alot libi bachoshech,
nirshamot achshav.

</td></tr>
<tr><td align="right">

אָנָּא, שְׁמֹר לִי עַל כָּל אֵלֶּה
וְעַל אֲהוּבֵי נַפְשִׁי,
עַל הַשֶּׁקֶט, עַל הַבֶּכִי
וְעַל זֶה הַשִּׁיר.
עַל כָּל אֵלֶּה...

</td><td>

Ana, shmor li al kol eileh
ve'al ahuvei nafshi,
al hasheket al habechi
ve'al ze hashir.
Al kol eileh...

</td></tr>
</table>

On the honey and on the sting
On the bitter and the sweet
On our baby daughter
Watch over and take care of them my good God

On the fire which is lit
On the pure water
On the man who returns home.

continued on next page

On all those, on all those
Please watch over for me my good God
On the honey and on the sting
On the bitter and sweet

Please don't uproot that which is planted
Don't forget the hope
Bring me back, and I shall return
To the good land.

Watch over my God on this house
On the garden on the wall
From sadness, from sudden fear
And from war

Watch over on the little I have
On the light and on the children
On the fruit that did not ripen
And wasn't yet picked.

And a star falls in its arc
All my dreams and my desires
Form crystal shapes out of the dark.

Guard for me, oh Lord, these treasures
All my friends keep safe and strong,
Guard the stillness, guard the weeping,
And above all, guard this song.

בשנה הבאה   *Bashana Haba-a*

Lyrics by Ehud Manor
Music: Nurit Hirsch

בַּשָּׁנָה הַבָּאָה נֵשֵׁב	Bashana haba-a neisheiv
עַל הַמִּרְפֶּסֶת	al ha-mirpeset
וְנִסְפֹּר צִפֳּרִים נוֹדְדוֹת.	v'nispor tziporim nod'dot.
יְלָדִים בְּחֻפְשָׁה יְשַׂחֲקוּ תּוֹפֶסֶת	Y'ladim b'chufsha y'sachaku tofeset
בֵּין הַבַּיִת לְבֵין הַשָּׂדוֹת.	bein habayit l'vein hasadot.
עוֹד תִּרְאֶה, עוֹד תִּרְאֶה	Od tir-eh od tir-eh
כַּמָּה טוֹב יִהְיֶה	kama tov yihyeh
בַּשָּׁנָה, בַּשָּׁנָה הַבָּאָה.	bashana bashana haba-a.
עֲנָבִים אֲדֻמִּים יַבְשִׁילוּ	Anavim adumim yavshilu
עַד הָעֶרֶב	ad ha-erev
וְיֻגְּשׁוּ צוֹנְנִים לַשֻּׁלְחָן;	v'yugshu tzon'nim lashulchan;
וְרוּחוֹת רְדוּמִים יִשְׂאוּ אֶל	v'ruchot r'dumin yis-u el
אֵם־הַדֶּרֶךְ	eim haderech
עִתּוֹנִים יְשָׁנִים וְעָנָן.	itonim y'shanim v'anan.
עוֹד תִּרְאֶה, עוֹד תִּרְאֶה...	Od tir-eh, od tir-eh...
בַּשָּׁנָה הַבָּאָה נִפְרֹשׂ	Bashana haba-a nifros
כַּפּוֹת־יָדַיִם	kapot yadayim
מוּל הָאוֹר הַנִּגָּר הַלָּבָן	mul ha-or hanigar halavan
אֲנָפָה לְבָנָה תִּפְרֹשׂ	anafa l'vana tifros
בָּאוֹר כְּנָפַיִם	ba-or k'nafayim
וְהַשֶּׁמֶשׁ תִּזְרַח בְּתוֹכָן.	v'hashemesh tizrach b'tochan.
עוֹד תִּרְאֶה, עוֹד תִּרְאֶה...	Od tir-eh, od tir-eh...

Next year, when peace will come,
we shall return to the simple pleasures of life
so long denied us.
　　You will see, you will see,
　　how good it will be—next year!

Next year we'll sit on the porch
And count migrating birds
Children on vacation will play tag
Between the house and the fields.
　　You will see...

Red grapes will ripen till the evening
And will be served chilled to the table.
And languid winds will carry to the crossroads
Old newspapers and a cloud.
　　You will see...

Next year we will spread out our hands
Towards the radiant light
A white heron like a light will spread her wings
And within them the sun will shine.
　　You will see...

ערב של שושנים *Erev Shel Shoshanim*

Lyrics: Moshe Dor
Music: Josef Hadar

עֶרֶב שֶׁל שׁוֹשַׁנִּים,
נֵצֵא־נָא אֶל הַבֻּסְתָּן,
מוֹר, בְּשָׂמִים וּלְבוֹנָה
לְרַגְלֵךְ מִפְתָּן.

Erev shel shoshanim,
Neitzei na el habustan,
Mor, b'samim u'l'vona
l'ragleich miftan.

לַיְלָה יוֹרֵד לְאַט
וְרוּחַ שׁוֹשָׁן נוֹשְׁבָה,
הָבָה אֶלְחַשׁ לָךְ שִׁיר בַּלָּאט,
זֶמֶר שֶׁל אַהֲבָה.

Laila yoreid l'at
v'ruach shoshan noshva,
hava elchash lach shir balat,
zemer shel ahava.

שַׁחַר, הוֹמָה יוֹנָה,
רֹאשֵׁךְ מָלֵא טְלָלִים,
פִּיךְ אֶל הַבֹּקֶר שׁוֹשַׁנָּה
אֶקְטְפֶנּוּ לִי.
לַיְלָה יוֹרֵד לְאַט...

Shachar homa yona,
rosheich malei t'lalim,
pich el haboker shoshana
eft'fenu li.
Laila yoreid l'at...

An evening of roses. Let us go out to the orchard;
Myrth, spices and frankincense shall be as a threshold for your feet.

The night comes upon us slowly and a breeze of roses is blowing;
Let me whisper a song to you quietly, a song of love.

It is dawn, a dove is cooing. Your hair is filled with dew;
Your lips are like a rose to the morning, I'll pick it for myself.

113

לָךְ יְרוּשָׁלַיִם   *Lach Y'rushalayim*

Lyrics: Amos Ettinger

Music: A. Rubinstein

לָךְ יְרוּשָׁלַיִם, בֵּין חוֹמוֹת הָעִיר

Lach Y'rushalayim bein chomot ha-ir,

לָךְ יְרוּשָׁלַיִם, אוֹר חָדָשׁ יָאִיר

Lach Y'rushalayim or chadash ya-ir.

בְּלִבֵּנוּ, רַק שִׁיר אֶחָד קַיָם

B'libeinu rak shir echad kayam

לָךְ יְרוּשָׁלַיִם, בֵּין

lach Y'rushalayim bein

יַרְדֵּן וָיָם

Yardein va-yam.

לָךְ יְרוּשָׁלַיִם, נוֹף

Lach Y'rushshalyim nof

קְדוּמִים וָהוֹד,

k'dumim va-hod,

לָךְ יְרוּשָׁלַיִם, לָךְ רָזִים וָסוֹד.

Lach Y'rushalayim lach razim va-sod.

בְּלִבֵּנוּ...

B'libeinu...

לָךְ יְרוּשָׁלַיִם, שִׁיר נִשָּׂא תָּמִיד,

Lach Y'rushalayim shir nisa tamid

לָךְ יְרוּשָׁלַיִם, עִיר מִגְדָּל-דָּוִד.

Lach Y'rushalayim ir Migdal David

בְּלִבֵּנוּ...

B'libeinu...

For you, O Jerusalem, fortress of David, let a new light shine.
In our hearts there exists but one song, a song dedicated to you.

For you Jerusalem, between the city walls,
For you Jerusalem, a new light will shine.

In our heart there exists but one song
For you Jerusalem, between the Jordan and the sea.

For you Jerusalem, an ancient glorious view,
For you Jerusalem a riddle and a secret.

שישו את ירושלים   Sisu Et Y'rushalayim

Lyrical sources: Isaiah 66:10, 62:6, 49:18, 60:21

ישעיה ס:י, סב:ו, מט:יח, ס:כא

Melody: Akiva Nof

שִׂישׂוּ אֶת יְרוּשָׁלַיִם, גִּילוּ בָהּ,
(גִּילוּ בָהּ) כָּל אֹהֲבֶיהָ.

Sisu et Y'rushalayim gilu va
(gilu va) kol ohaveha kol ohaveha

עַל חוֹמוֹתַיִךְ עִיר דָּוִד
הִפְקַדְתִּי שׁוֹמְרִים
כָּל־הַיּוֹם וְכָל־הַלָּיְלָה.

Al chomotayich ir David
hif-kad-ti shomrim
kol hayom v'chol halaila.

שִׂישׂוּ אֶת יְרוּשָׁלַיִם...   *Sisu et Y'rushalayim...*

אַל תִּירָא וְאַל תֵּחַת עַבְדִּי
יַעֲקֹב, כִּי יָפֻצוּ מְשַׂנְאֶיךָ
מִפָּנֶיךָ

Al tira v'al teichat avdi
Ya-akov, ki yafutzu m'sanecha
mipanecha.

שִׂישׂוּ אֶת יְרוּשָׁלַיִם...   *Sisu et Y'rushalayim...*

שְׂאִי סָבִיב עֵינַיִךְ וּרְאִי כֻּלָּם
נִקְבְּצוּ וּבָאוּ לָךְ.

S'i saviv einayich ur'I kulam,
nik-b'tzu u-va-u lach.

שִׂישׂוּ אֶת יְרוּשָׁלַיִם...   *Sisu et Y'rushalayim...*

וְעַמֵּךְ כֻּלָּם צַדִּיקִים
לְעוֹלָם יִירְשׁוּ אָרֶץ.

V'ameich kulam tzadikim
l'olam yirshu aretz.

שִׂישׂוּ אֶת יְרוּשָׁלַיִם...   *Sisu et Y'rushalayim...*

Rejoice with Jerusalem, all you who love her.
I have set watchmen upon thy walls, O Jerusalem.
They shall never hold their peace, day or night.

Do not fear, my servant Jacob,
For your enemies shall be scattered before you.
Look about you and behold; they are gathering and coming unto you.

And your people are all holy and forever shall inherit the land.

ירושלים של זהב Y'rushalayim Shel Zahav

Music and lyrics: Naomi Shemer.

אֲוִיר־הָרִים צָלוּל כַּיַּיִן
וְרֵיחַ אֳרָנִים,
נִשָּׂא בְּרוּחַ הָעַרְבַּיִם
עִם קוֹל פַּעֲמוֹנִים.

Avir harim tzalul kayayin
v'reiach oranim,
nisa beru'ach ha'arbayim
im kol pa'amonim.

וּבְתַרְדֵּמַת אִילָן וָאֶבֶן,
שְׁבוּיָה בַּחֲלוֹמָהּ
הָעִיר אֲשֶׁר בָּדָד יוֹשֶׁבֶת,
וּבְלִבָּהּ חוֹמָה.

Uvetardemat ilan va'even,
shvuyah bachalomah,
ha'ir asher badad yoshevet,
uvelibah chomah.

יְרוּשָׁלַיִם שֶׁל זָהָב
וְשֶׁל נְחֹשֶׁת וְשֶׁל אוֹר
הֲלֹא לְכָל שִׁירַיִךְ
אֲנִי כִּנּוֹר.

Y'rushalayim shel zahav
veshel nechoshet veshel or
halo lechol shirayich
ani kinor.

Verses added after 1967:

חָזַרְנוּ אֶל בּוֹרוֹת הַמַּיִם
לַשּׁוּק וְלַכִּכָּר
שׁוֹפָר קוֹרֵא בְּהַר הַבַּיִת
בָּעִיר הָעַתִּיקָה.

Chazarnu el borot hamayim
lashuk velakikar,
shofar kore behar habayit
ba'ir ha'atikah.

וּבַמְּעָרוֹת אֲשֶׁר בַּסֶּלַע
אַלְפֵי שְׁמָשׁוֹת זוֹרְחוֹת
נָשׁוּב נֵרֵד אֶל יָם הַמֶּלַח
בְּדֶרֶךְ יְרִיחוֹ.
ירושלים של זהב...

Uvame'arot asher baselah
alfei shmashot zorchot,
nashuv nered el yam hamelach
b'derech Yericho!
Y'rushalayim shel zahav...

אַךְ בְּבוֹאִי הַיּוֹם לָשִׁיר לָךְ
וְלָךְ לִקְשׁוֹר כְּתָרִים,
קָטֹנְתִּי מִצְּעִיר בָּנַיִךְ
וּמֵאַחֲרוֹן הַמְשׁוֹרְרִים.

Ach bevo'i hayom lashir lach
v'lach lik'shor k'tarim,
katonti mitze'ir bana'ich
ume'acharon ham'shorerim.

כִּי שְׁמֵךְ צוֹרֵב אֶת הַשְּׂפָתַיִם
כִּנְשִׁיקַת שָׂרָף.
אִם אֶשְׁכָּחֵךְ יְרוּשָׁלַיִם
אֲשֶׁר כֻּלָּהּ זָהָב...
ירושלים של זהב...

Ki shmech tzorev et hasfatayim
keneshikat saraf,
im eshkachech Yerushalayim
asher kulah zahav...
Y'rushalayim shel zahav...

The mountain air is clear as wine and the scent of pines
is carried on the breeze of twilight with the sound of bells.

And in the slumber of tree and stone captured in her dream
The city that sits solitary and in its midst is a wall.

Jerusalem of gold and of bronze, and of light
behold I am a violin for all your songs.

We have returned to the cisterns to the market and to the market-place
a ram's horn calls out on the Temple Mount in the Old City.

And in the caves in the mountain thousands of suns shine
we will once again descend to the Dead Sea by way of Jericho!

But as I come to sing to you today, and to adorn crowns to you (to tell your
praise) I am the smallest of the youngest of your children (the least worthy
of doing so) and of the last poet (of all the poets born).

For your name scorches the lips like the kiss of a seraph
if I forget thee, Jerusalem, which is all gold...

Jerusalem of gold...

הדלקת נרות חנוכה Chanukah Candle Lighting

The Chanukah blessings are recited before the candles are lit. On Friday evening, candles are lit before the Shabbat candles and on Saturday evening, following Havdalah. The candles are placed right-to-left and lit left-to-right. It is customary to leave the Chanukiah by a window to "advertise" the miracle of Chanukah.

בָּרוּךְ אַתָּה יי אֱלֹהֵינוּ מֶלֶךְ
הָעוֹלָם, אֲשֶׁר קִדְּשָׁנוּ בְּמִצְוֹתָיו,
וְצִוָּנוּ לְהַדְלִיק נֵר שֶׁל חֲנֻכָּה.

Baruch atah Adonai Eloheinu melech
ha-olam, asher kid'shanu b'mitzvotav,
v'tzivanu l'hadlik ner shel Chanukah.

Praised are You, Lord our God, Sovereign of the universe, who has sanctified us with God's commandments and commanded us to light the Chanukah light.

בָּרוּךְ אַתָּה יי אֱלֹהֵינוּ מֶלֶךְ
הָעוֹלָם, שֶׁעָשָׂה נִסִּים לַאֲבוֹתֵינוּ
בַּיָּמִים הָהֵם וּבַזְּמַן הַזֶּה.

Baruch atah Adonai Eloheinu melech
ha-olam, she'asa nisim l'avoteinu
bayamim haheim u'vazman hazeh.

Praised are You, Lord our God, Sovereign of the universe, who accomplished miracles for our ancestors in ancient days and in our time.

First night only:

בָּרוּךְ אַתָּה יְיָ אֱלֹהֵינוּ מֶלֶךְ
הָעוֹלָם, שֶׁהֶחֱיָנוּ וְקִיְּמָנוּ
וְהִגִּיעָנוּ לַזְּמַן הַזֶּה.

Baruch atah Adonai Eloheinu melech
ha-olam, shehecheyanu v'ki-manu
v'higi-anu laz'man hazeh.

Praised are You, Lord our God, Sovereign of the universe, who has kept us in life, sustained us and enabled us to reach this season.

On all nights, following candle lighting:

הנרות הללו אנחנו מדליקים   *Haneirot halalu anachnu madlikin*

הַנֵּרוֹת הַלָּלוּ אֲנַחְנוּ מַדְלִיקִים
עַל הַנִּסִּים וְעַל הַנִּפְלָאוֹת וְעַל

Haneirot halalu anachnu madlikin
al ha nisim v'al ha-nifla'ot v'al

118

הַתְּשׁוּעוֹת וְעַל הַמִּלְחָמוֹת, hat'shu'ot v'al ha milchamot,
שֶׁעָשִׂיתָ לַאֲבוֹתֵינוּ בַּיָּמִים she-a-sita la'avoteinu bayamim
הָהֵם בַּזְּמַן הַזֶּה, עַל יְדֵי haheim bazman ha-zeh, al y'dci
כֹּהֲנֶיךָ הַקְּדוֹשִׁים. kohanecha hak'doshim.

וְכָל־שְׁמוֹנַת יְמֵי חֲנֻכָּה V'chol shmonat y'mei Chanukah
הַנֵּרוֹת הַלָּלוּ קֹדֶשׁ הֵם, וְאֵין haneirot halalu kodesh heim, v'ein
לָנוּ רְשׁוּת לְהִשְׁתַּמֵּשׁ בָּהֶם, lanu reshut l'hishtameish baheim,
אֶלָּא לִרְאוֹתָם בִּלְבַד, כְּדֵי elah lir'otam bilvad, k'dei
לְהוֹדוֹת וּלְהַלֵּל לְשִׁמְךָ הַגָּדוֹל, l'hodot ul'hallel l'shimcha hagadol,
עַל נִסֶּיךָ וְעַל נִפְלְאוֹתֶיךָ וְעַל al nisecha v'al nifl'otecha v'al
יְשׁוּעָתֶךָ. y'shuatecha.

These lights we kindle to recall the wondrous triumphs and the miraculous victories wrought through Your holy priests for our ancestors in ancient days at this season. These lights are sacred throughout all days of Chanukah. We may not put them to ordinary use, but are to look upon them and thus be reminded to thank and praise You for Your wondrous miracle of our deliverance.

מעוז צור *Ma'oz Tzur*

מָעוֹז צוּר יְשׁוּעָתִי Ma'oz tzur yeshu'ati
לְךָ נָאֶה לְשַׁבֵּחַ, lecha na'eh l'shabei'ach,
תִּכּוֹן בֵּית תְּפִלָּתִי tikon beit tefilati
וְשָׁם תּוֹדָה נְזַבֵּחַ, vesham todah nezabei'ach,
לְעֵת תָּכִין מַטְבֵּחַ le'et tachin matbei'ach
מִצָּר הַמְּנַבֵּחַ, mitzar ham'nabei'ach,
אָז אֶגְמֹר בְּשִׁיר מִזְמוֹר az egmor b'shir mizmor
חֲנֻכַּת הַמִּזְבֵּחַ. Chanukat hamizbei'ach.

Rock of Ages, let our song praise Your saving power. You amid the raging throng were our sheltering tower. Furious they assailed us, but Your help availed us. And Your word broke their sword when our own strength failed us.

הבדלה   *Havdalah*

For the conclusion of Shabbat. (At the conclusion of a Festival, begin with the blessing over wine and omit blessings over the spices and candle.)

אליהו הנביא   *Eliyahu Hanavi*

אֵלִיָּהוּ הַנָּבִיא, אֵלִיָּהוּ הַתִּשְׁבִּי,

אֵלִיָּהוּ, אֵלִיָּהוּ, אֵלִיָּהוּ הַגִּלְעָדִי.

Eliyahu Hanavi, Eliyahu hatishbi,
Eliyahu, Eliyahu, Eliyahu ha-Gil-adi.

בִּמְהֵרָה בְיָמֵנוּ יָבוֹא אֵלֵינוּ

עִם מָשִׁיחַ בֶּן דָּוִד,

עִם מָשִׁיחַ בֶּן דָּוִד.

Bimheira v'yameinu yavo eileinu,
im Mashiach ben David,
im Mashiach ben David.

May the Prophet Elijah come soon,
In our time, with Messiah, son of David.

Leader, holding a cup of wine/grape juice:

הִנֵּה אֵל יְשׁוּעָתִי, אֶבְטַח וְלֹא
אֶפְחָד, כִּי עָזִּי וְזִמְרָת יָהּ יְיָ,
וַיְהִי־לִי לִישׁוּעָה. וּשְׁאַבְתֶּם־
מַיִם בְּשָׂשׂוֹן, מִמַּעַיְנֵי הַיְשׁוּעָה.
לַיְיָ הַיְשׁוּעָה, עַל עַמְּךָ
בִרְכָתֶךָ סֶּלָה. יְיָ צְבָאוֹת
עִמָּנוּ, מִשְׂגָּב לָנוּ אֱלֹהֵי יַעֲקֹב
סֶלָה. יְיָ צְבָאוֹת, אַשְׁרֵי אָדָם
בֹּטֵחַ בָּךְ. יְיָ הוֹשִׁיעָה,
הַמֶּלֶךְ יַעֲנֵנוּ בְיוֹם קָרְאֵנוּ.

Hinei Eil y'shu-ati, evtach v'lo
efchad, ki ozi v'zimrat yah Adonai,
va-y'hi li lishu-a. U'shavtem
mayim b'sason mima-ai-nei hay-shu-a.
Ladonai hay-shu-a, al amcha
birchatecha sela. Adonai tz'va-ot
imanu, misgav lanu elohei Ya-akov,
sela, Adonai tz'va-ot, ashrei adam
botei-ach bach. Adonai hoshia,
hamelech ya-aneinu v'yom koreinu.

Recite bolded lines all together

לַיְּהוּדִים הָיְתָה אוֹרָה וְשִׂמְחָה
וְשָׂשׂוֹן וִיקָר. כֵּן תִּהְיֶה לָּנוּ.
כּוֹס־יְשׁוּעוֹת אֶשָּׂא וּבְשֵׁם יְיָ
אֶקְרָא.

**La-y'hudim ha-y'ta ora v'simcha,
v'sason vicar. Kein tihyeh lanu.**
Kos y'shu'ot esa, uv-sheim Adonai
ekra.

ישעיה יב: ב-ג, תהילים ג:ט, מו:יב,
כ:י פד:יג, אסתר ח:טז, תהילים קטז:יג

Isaiah 12:2-3; Psalms 3:9, 46:12, 84:13; 20:10;
Esther 8:16; Psalms 116:13

Behold, God is my unfailing help;
I will trust in God and will not be afraid.
The Lord is my strength and song;
The Lord is my Deliverer.
With joy shall you draw water
out of the wells of salvation.
The Lord alone is our help;
May the Lord bless the Lord's people.
The Lord of the universe is with us;
The God of Jacob is our protection.

Adonai tzva'ot.
Blessed is the one who trusts in You.
Help us, Lord; answer us, O King when we call

There was light and joy,
Gladness and honor for the Jewish people.
So may we be blessed.
I will lift the cup of salvation,
And call upon the name of the Lord.

For wine/grape juice:

סַבְרִי מָרָנָן:

Savri maranan:

בָּרוּךְ אַתָּה יי אֱלֹהֵינוּ מֶלֶךְ

Baruch atah Adonai Eloheinu melech

הָעוֹלָם, בּוֹרֵא פְּרִי הַגֶּפֶן.

ha-olam, borei p'ri hagafen.

Praised are You, Lord our God, Sovereign of the universe,
Creator of the fruit of the vine.

If wine or grape juice is not available, use any other beverage:

בָּרוּךְ אַתָּה יְיָ אֱלֹהֵינוּ מֶלֶךְ

Baruch atah Adonai Eloheinu melech

הָעוֹלָם, שֶׁהַכֹּל נִהְיֶה בִּדְבָרוֹ.

ha-olam, shehakol n'hiyeh bidvaro.

Praised are You, Lord Our God, Sovereign of the universe
at whose word all things come into being.

121

After the following blessing, inhale the spices:

בָּרוּךְ אַתָּה יי אֱלֹהֵינוּ מֶלֶךְ
הָעוֹלָם, בּוֹרֵא מִינֵי בְשָׂמִים.

Baruch atah Adonai Eloheinu melech
ha-olam, borei minei v'samim.

Praised are You, Lord our God, Sovereign of the universe,
Creator of various spices.

The hands are cupped and extended toward the Havdalah candle:

בָּרוּךְ אַתָּה יי אֱלֹהֵינוּ מֶלֶךְ
הָעוֹלָם, בּוֹרֵא מְאוֹרֵי הָאֵשׁ.

Baruch atah Adonai Eloheinu melech
ha-olam, borei m'orei ha-eish.

Praised are You, Lord our God, Sovereign of the universe,
Creator of the light of fire.

Leader, raising the cup of wine again:

בָּרוּךְ אַתָּה יי אֱלֹהֵינוּ מֶלֶךְ
הָעוֹלָם, הַמַּבְדִּיל בֵּין קֹדֶשׁ
לְחוֹל, בֵּין אוֹר לְחֹשֶׁךְ, בֵּין
יִשְׂרָאֵל לָעַמִּים, בֵּין יוֹם
הַשְּׁבִיעִי לְשֵׁשֶׁת יְמֵי הַמַּעֲשֶׂה.
בָּרוּךְ אַתָּה יי, הַמַּבְדִּיל בֵּין
קֹדֶשׁ לְחוֹל.

Baruch atah Adonai Eloheinu melech
ha-olam, hamavdil bein kodesh
l'chol, bein or l'choshech, bein
Yisrael la-amin, bein yom
hashvi-i l'sheishet y'mei hama-aseh.
Baruch atah Adonai, hamavdil bein
kodesh l'chol.

Praised are You, Lord our God, Sovereign of the universe, who has made a
distinction between the holy and the ordinary, between light and darkness,
between the people of Israel and all other nations of the world, between the
seventh day and the six ordinary days of the week. Praised are You, O Lord,
who has made a distinction between the holy and the ordinary.

Drink from the wine cup (some add the word in parentheses).

הַמַּבְדִּיל בֵּין קֹדֶשׁ לְחוֹל,
חַטֹּאתֵינוּ הוּא יִמְחֹל.
זַרְעֵנוּ וְכַסְפֵּנוּ (וּשְׁלוֹמֵנוּ)
יַרְבֶּה כַחוֹל, וְכַכּוֹכָבִים בַּלָּיְלָה.

Hamavdil bein kodesh l'chol,
chatoteinu hu yimchol.
Zareinu v'chaspeinu (ush'lomeinu)
yarbeh kachol, v'chakochavim balaila.

122

God separates sacred and profane; May God forgive our transgressions, and make our people as numerous as the sand, and as the stars of the night.

שָׁבוּעַ טוֹב!   *Shavua tov!*

A Good Week!

התקוה   *Hatikva*

כָּל עוֹד בַּלֵּבָב פְּנִימָה,	Kol od baleivav p'nima,
נֶפֶשׁ יְהוּדִי הוֹמִיָּה.	nefesh y'hudi homiya.
וּלְפַאֲתֵי מִזְרָח קָדִימָה,	Ul-fa-atei mizrach kadima,
עַיִן לְצִיּוֹן צוֹפִיָּה.	ayin l'tzion tzofiyah.
עוֹד לֹא אָבְדָה תִקְוָתֵנוּ,	Od lo av'da tikvateinu,
הַתִּקְוָה בַּת שְׁנוֹת אַלְפַּיִם,	hatikva bat sh'not alpayim,
לִהְיוֹת עַם חָפְשִׁי בְּאַרְצֵנוּ	lih-yot am chofshi b'artzeinu
אֶרֶץ צִיּוֹן וִירוּשָׁלַיִם.	eretz Tzion Virushalayim.

As long as in the heart within
A Jewish soul still yearns,
And onward, toward the end of the east,
An eye still gazes toward Zion.

Our hope is not yet lost,
The hope of two thousand years,
To be a free people in our land
The land of Zion and Jerusalem.

תפילת הדרך T'filat HaDerech
(Prayer for Travelers)

The phrase in parentheses is recited if one plans to return to this location in the near future, otherwise, recite entire text prior to departure.

יְהִי רָצוֹן מִלְּפָנֶיךָ, יי
אֱלֹהֵינוּ וֵאלֹהֵי אֲבוֹתֵינוּ,
שֶׁתּוֹלִיכֵנוּ לְשָׁלוֹם, וְתַצְעִידֵנוּ
לְשָׁלוֹם, וְתַדְרִיכֵנוּ לְשָׁלוֹם,
וְתִסְמְכֵנוּ לְשָׁלוֹם, וְתַגִּיעֵנוּ
לִמְחוֹז חֶפְצֵנוּ לְחַיִּים וּלְשִׂמְחָה
וּלְשָׁלוֹם, (וְתַחֲזִירֵנוּ לְבֵיתֵנוּ
לְשָׁלוֹם). וְתַצִּילֵנוּ מִכַּף
כָּל־אוֹיֵב, וְאוֹרֵב וְאָסוֹן בַּדֶּרֶךְ,
וּמִכָּל מִינֵי פֻּרְעָנִיּוֹת
הַמִּתְרַגְּשׁוֹת לָבוֹא לָעוֹלָם.
וְתִשְׁלַח בְּרָכָה בְּמַעֲשֵׂה יָדֵינוּ,
וְתִתְּנֵנוּ לְחֵן וּלְחֶסֶד
וּלְרַחֲמִים בְּעֵינֶיךָ וּבְעֵינֵי
כָל־רוֹאֵינוּ, וְתִשְׁמַע קוֹל
תַּחֲנוּנֵינוּ, כִּי אֵל שׁוֹמֵעַ תְּפִלָּה
וְתַחֲנוּן אָתָּה. בָּרוּךְ אַתָּה יי,
שׁוֹמֵעַ תְּפִלָּה.

Y'hi ratzon mil'fanecha Adonai
Eloheinu veilohei avoteinu,
shetolicheinu l'shalom, v'tatzideinu
l'shalom v'tadricheinu l'shalom
v'tismecheinu l'shalom v'tagi-einu
limchoz cheftzeinu l'chayim ul-simcha
ul-shalom, (v'tachazireinu l'veiteinu
l'shalom). V'tatzileinu mikaf
kol oyeiv v'oreiv, v'ason baderech,
u'mikol minei pur'aniyot
hamitragshot lavo la'olam.
V'tishlach bracha b'ma'asei yadeinu,
v'titneinu l'chein ul'chesed
ul'rachamim b'einecha u'veinei
chol roeinu, v'tishma kol
tachanuneinu, ki El shomei'a tefilah
v'tachanun atah. Baruch atah Adonai,
shomei-a t'fila.

May it be Your will, Lord our God and God of our ancestors, to lead us on the way of peace, so that You will bring us happily to our destination safe and sound. Save us from danger on the way. Give us good grace, kindness and favor both in Your eyes and in the eyes of all we may meet. Hear our prayer for You are a God who listens to the heart's supplication. Praised are You, Lord, who hears our prayers.